FUN EXPERIMENTS WITH SCIENCE

on Looking

Roy Richards

GW01464501

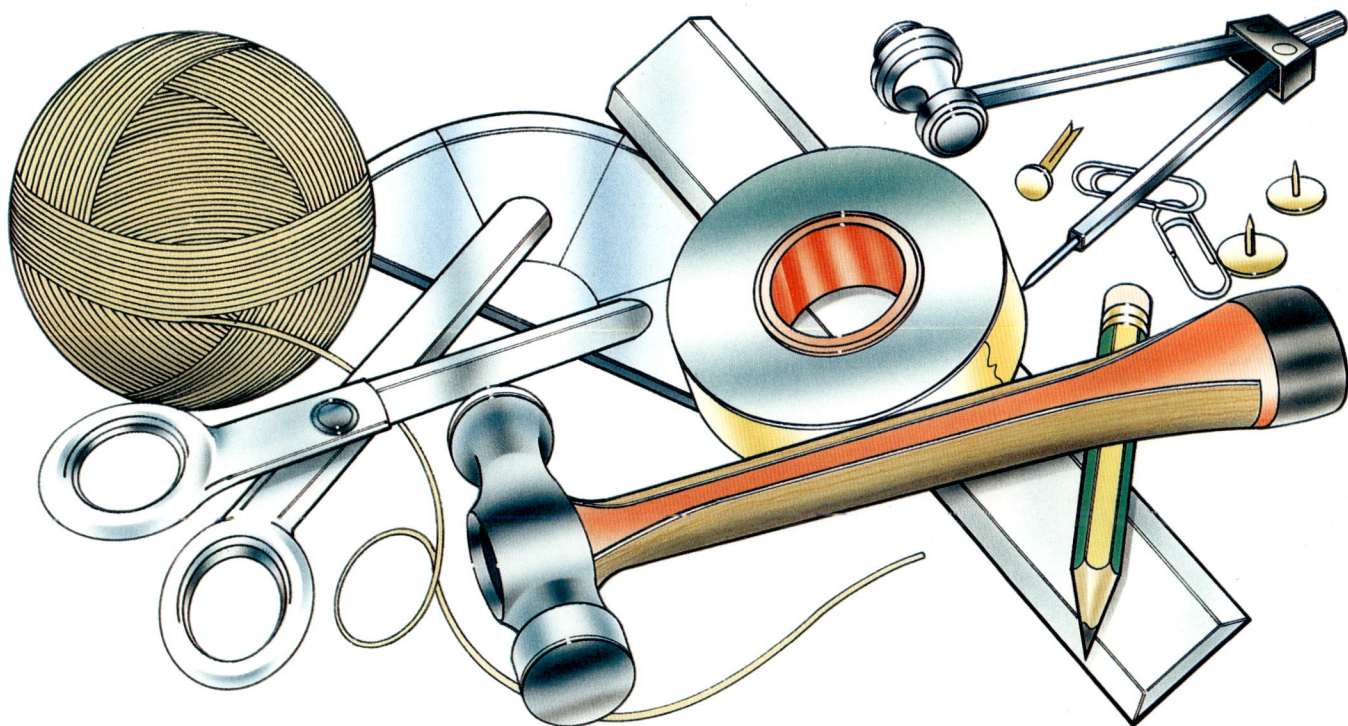

SIMON & SCHUSTER

LONDON • SYDNEY • NEW YORK • TOKYO • SINGAPORE • TORONTO

Contents

First published in 1990
by Simon & Schuster Young Books

Simon & Schuster Young Books
Simon & Schuster Ltd
Wolsey House, Wolsey Road
Hemel Hempstead, Herts HP2 4SS

Text © 1990 Roy Richards
Illustrations © 1990 Simon & Schuster

All rights reserved

Designed by David West
Children's Book Design
Illustrated by Alex Pang

Printed and bound in Belgium
by Proost International Book Production

British Library Cataloguing in Publication
Data
Richards, Roy
  On looking.
  1. Science. Experiments
  I. Title   II. Series
  507.24

ISBN 0–7500–0282–4

MIRROR PLAY

Use a mirror.

1 Look at the sky. Be careful. Do not look at the sun.

2 Look around corners with your mirror.

3 Look behind you. What can you see.

4 Use your mirror to look over walls.

5 Write your name on a large piece of paper. Look at it in a mirror.

JUST ONE MIRROR

Take a handbag mirror.

Put it along each dotted line in turn, shiny side facing each picture, as shown in the picture on the left. What happens?

Make some designs of your own.

Put your mirror here

DICK

MARY

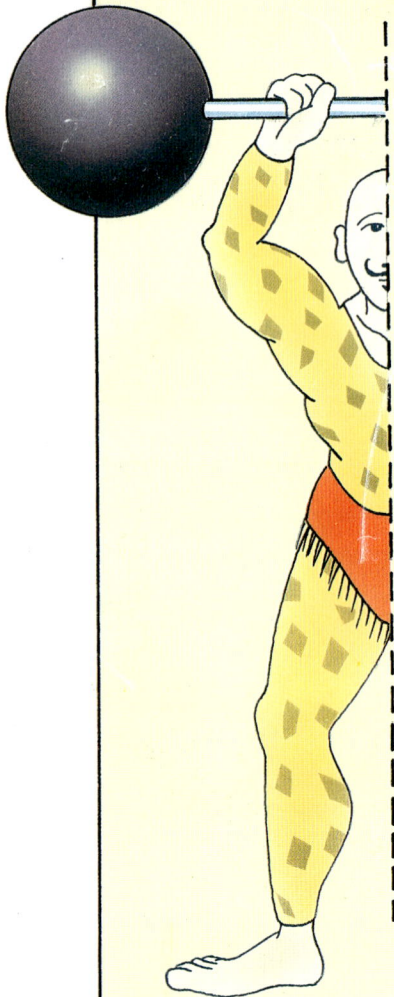

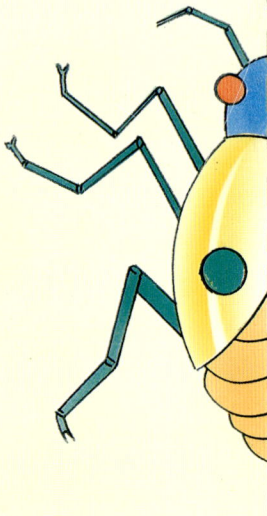

1 Try your mirror on letters.

2 Examine the letters of the alphabet below. Which have vertical symmetry? Which have horizontal symmetry? Which have both? Which have none? Use the letters that show symmetry to make symmetrical words as shown below at the bottom of the page.

Put your mirror vertically down the centre of the letter A.

The letter A has vertical symmetry.

Try it on the letter B.

It does not work for the letter B.

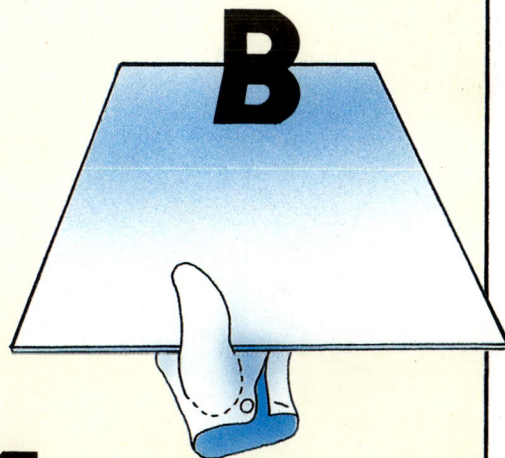

ABCDE FGHIJK LMNOP QRSTU VWXYZ

Try the mirror horizontally across the letter B.

Now it works! The letter B has horizontal symmetry.

H A T

MUM

symmetrical words

CHOICE

TRY TWO MIRRORS

1 Join two mirrors with sticky tape as below.

2 Stand them up with the mirror fronts facing you.

3 Try your mirrors on each tortoise in turn. Place the mirrors on the dotted lines as shown, shiny sides facing on the tortoise. What happens? Now try these patterns.

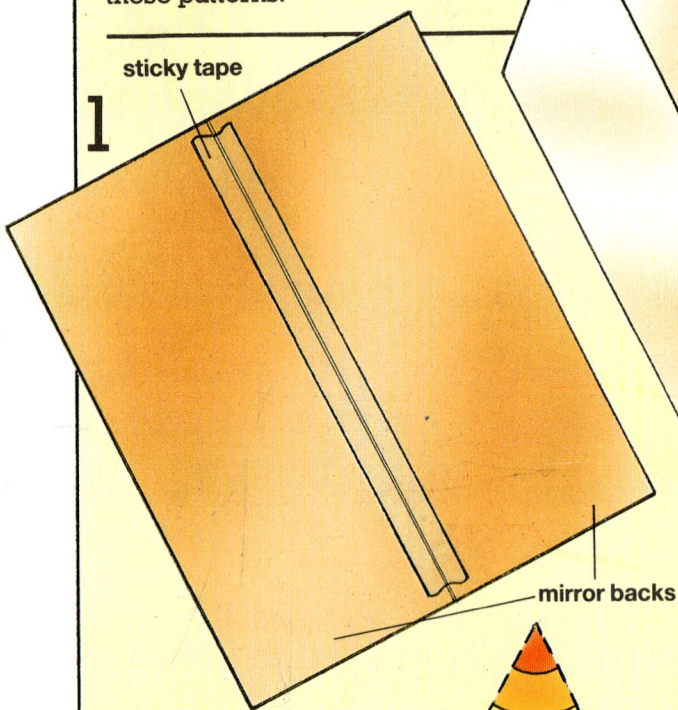

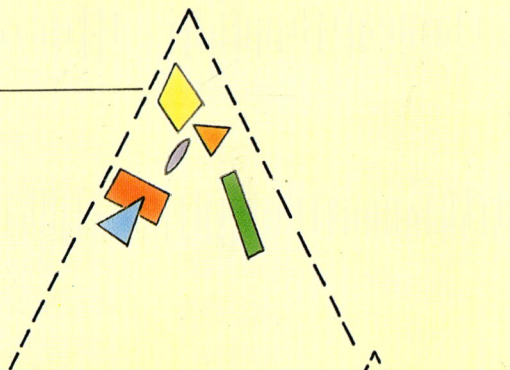

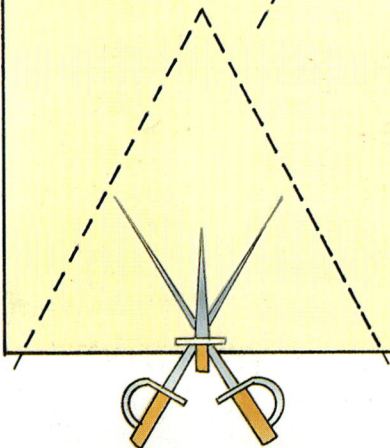

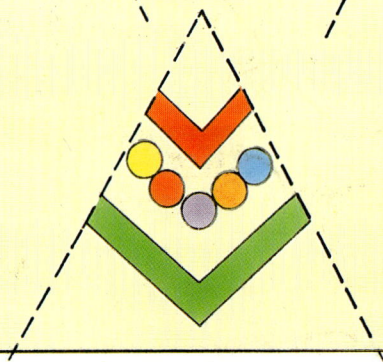

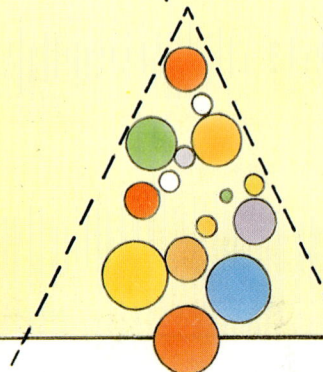

3 place your mirrors here, shiny sides facing tortoise

2

1

sticky tape

mirror fronts

mirror backs

patterns

KALEIDOSCOPE

It is easiest to use three mirrors to make a kaleidoscope.

1 Place your mirrors onto two pieces of masking tape, shiny surface up.

2 Turn the two side mirrors up to form a triangular prism. Tape the top edge. This is your kaleidoscope

Angle the kaleidoscope to look at different things in the room.

Can you make different patterns?

3 Now cover one end of the kaleidoscope with a piece of clear plastic cut from a plastic bag.

4 Hold it in place with an elastic band.

5 Put coloured pieces of card into your kaleidoscope. Cover the open end with a piece of greaseproof paper. Stick the edge with masking tape or sticky tape.

Hold the kaleidoscope to the light. Rotate it to see the pattern.

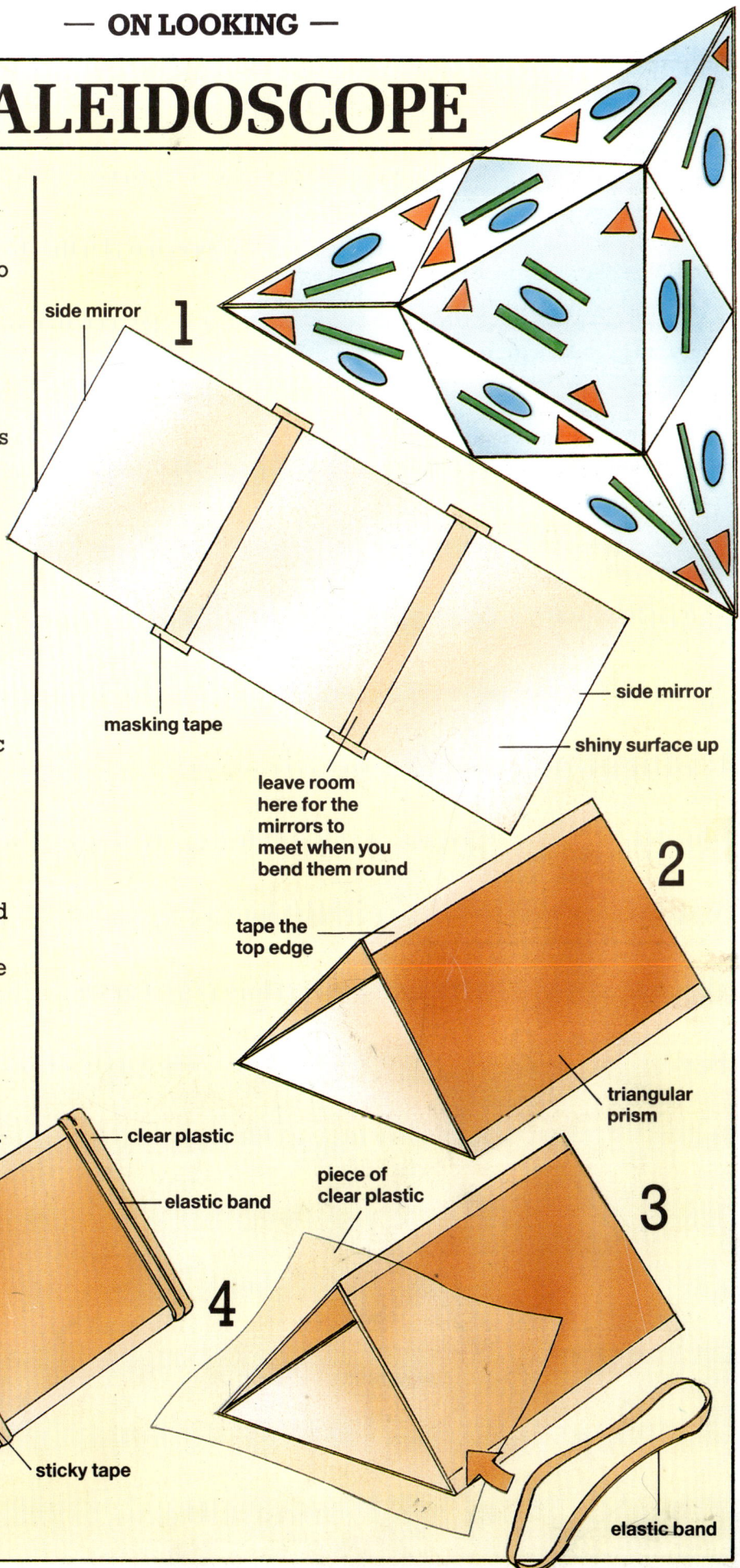

1
side mirror

masking tape

leave room here for the mirrors to meet when you bend them round

side mirror

shiny surface up

2
tape the top edge

triangular prism

clear plastic

elastic band

piece of clear plastic

3

4

5
coloured pieces of card

greaseproof paper

sticky tape

elastic band

PERISCOPES

Periscopes can be used to peep over walls or around corners. They can also be used to watch processions.

You will need two handbag mirrors to make a periscope and some long pieces of card.

1 Cut a long piece of card about 3 times as long as the mirror but just as wide. Tape one of your mirrors to one end of the piece of card, with the shiny surface facing up.

2 Fold the card into a triangular prism. Make sure you have a 90 degree angle at one corner. You may have a slight overlap in the card. Tape this overlap.

3 Do the same thing with your other mirror.

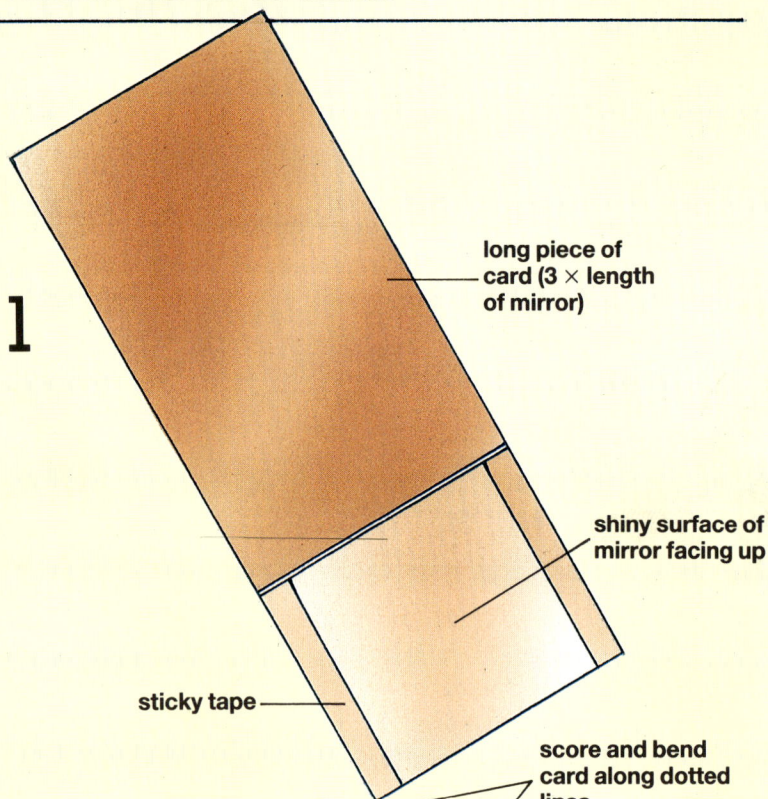

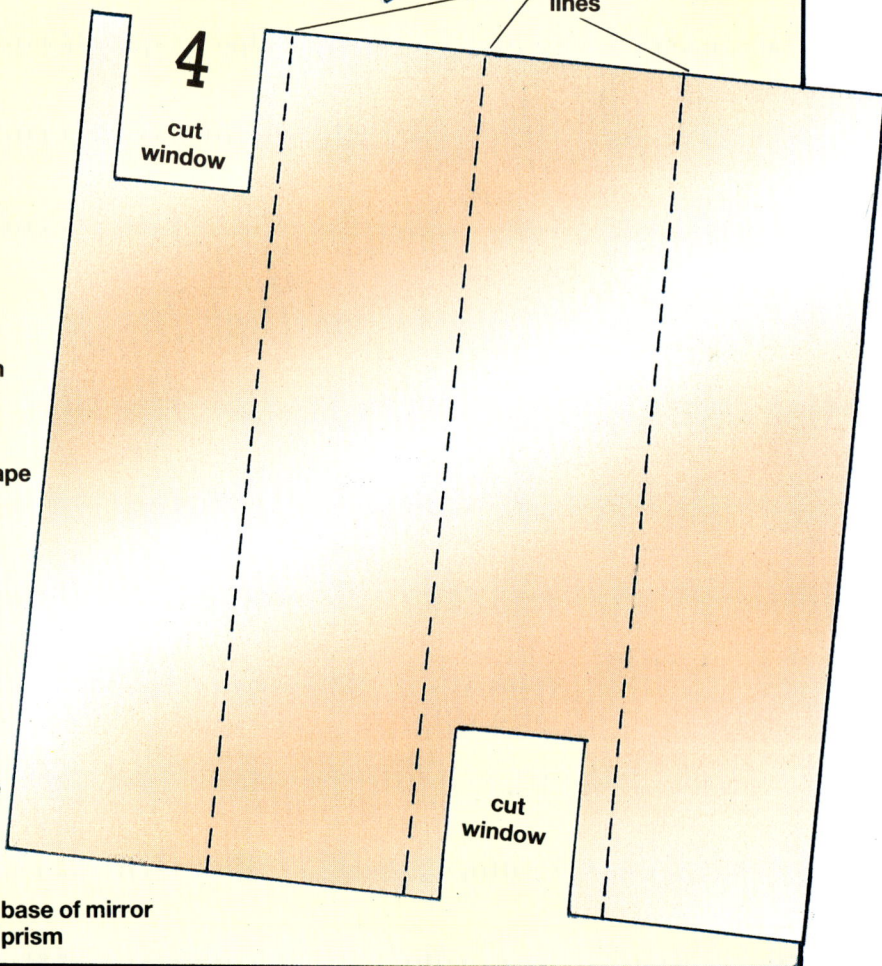

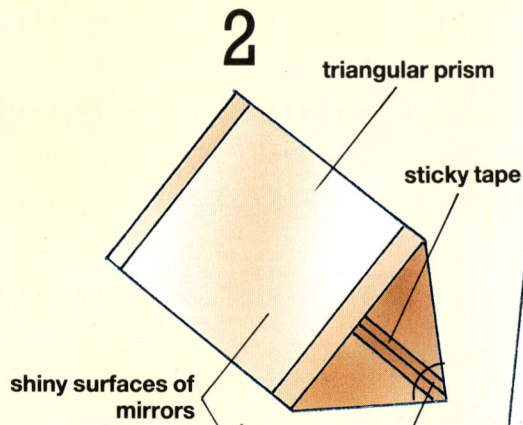

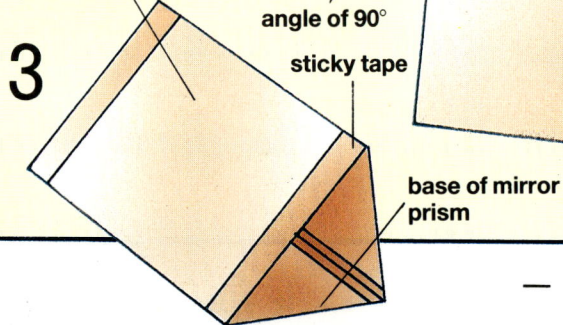

1

long piece of card (3 × length of mirror)

shiny surface of mirror facing up

sticky tape

4

score and bend card along dotted lines

cut window

cut window

2

triangular prism

sticky tape

shiny surfaces of mirrors

angle of 90°

3

sticky tape

base of mirror prism

4 Cut another long piece of card as shown in the picture on the bottom right of page 8. Score your card and bend it. Cut two windows. You are going to fold this to make the long tube shown in the two pictures below.

5 Make the long tube shown on the right. Its width and depth must be the same as that of the base of your mirror prism. Hold the edges with tape.

6 Put each triangular prism into the card tube so that the shiny surface of the mirror faces the window. Tape it in place.

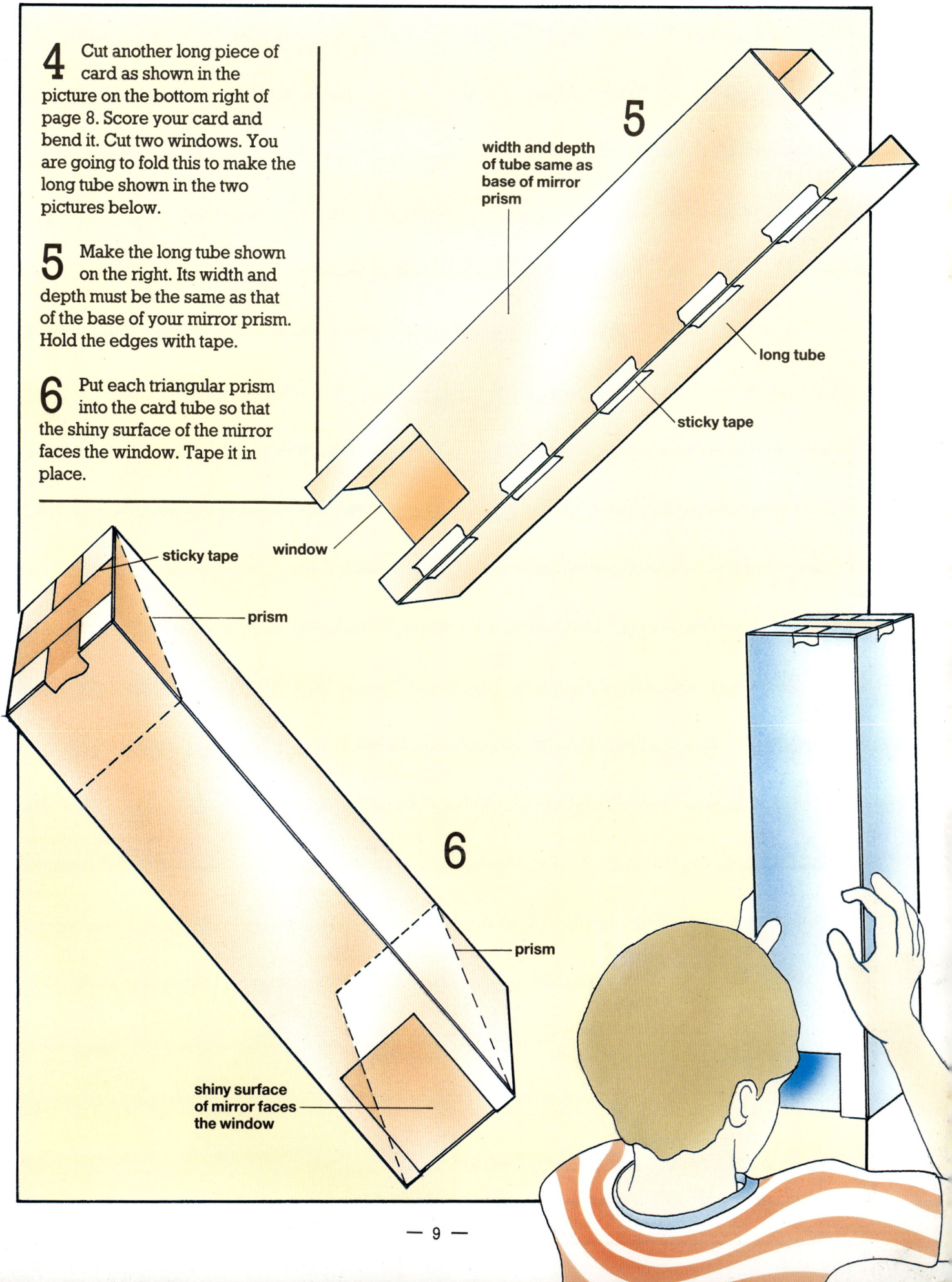

5

width and depth of tube same as base of mirror prism

long tube

sticky tape

window

sticky tape

prism

6

prism

shiny surface of mirror faces the window

SEEING IS BELIEVING

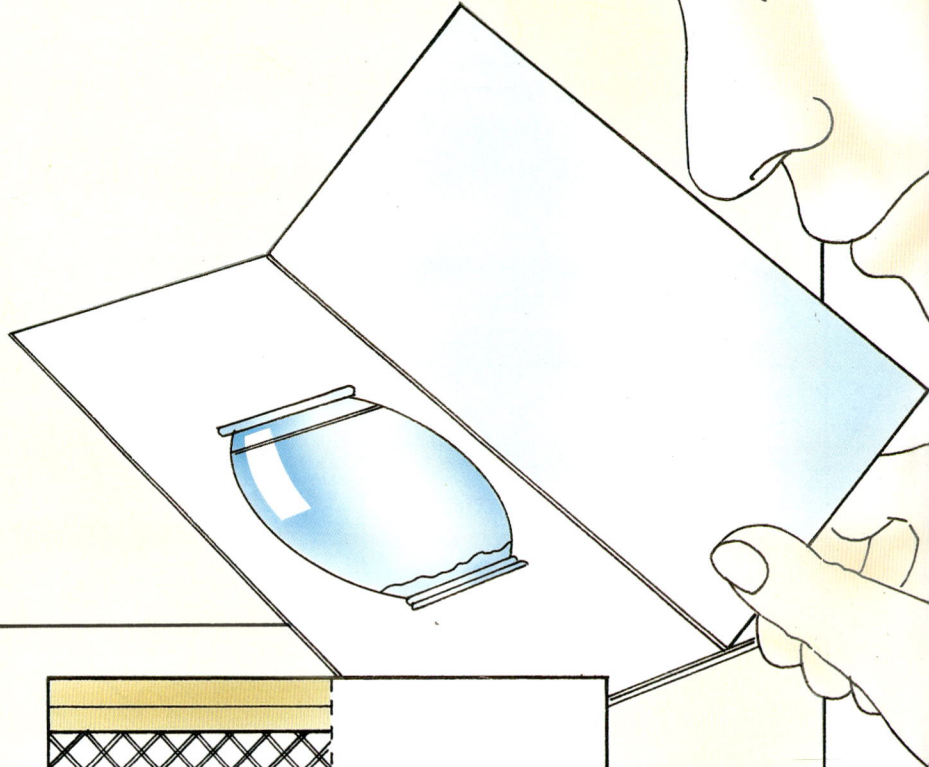

1 Cut out a piece of card the same size as the one immediately below.

2 Place your card vertically along the dotted line between each of the pictures below. Put your nose on the top edge of the card as shown in the picture on the right. What happens?

Each eye receives a separate image. The brain merges these two images to make one picture. So the rabbit pops into its hutch or the spider into its web.

card

70mm

45mm

place your card vertically along the dotted line

Make up some illusion cards.

Try them on your friends.

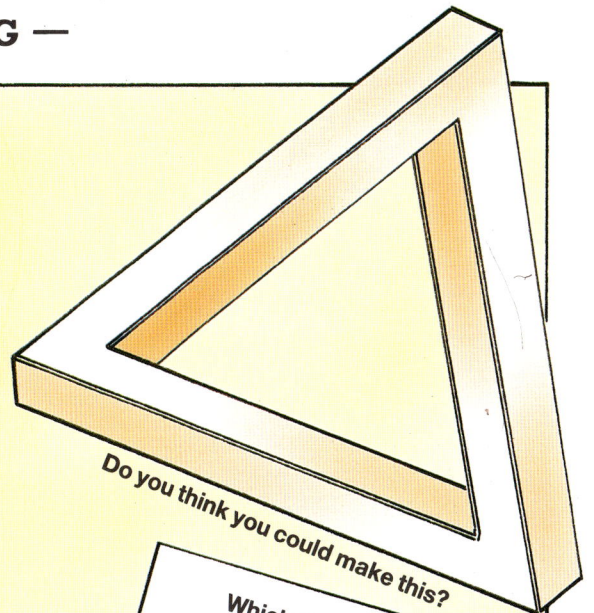

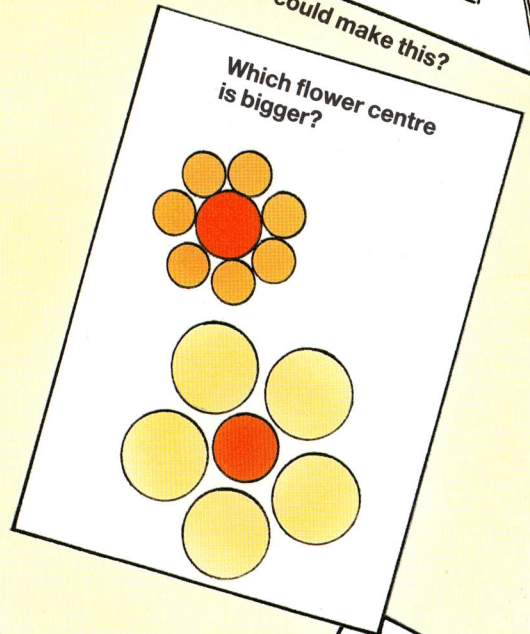

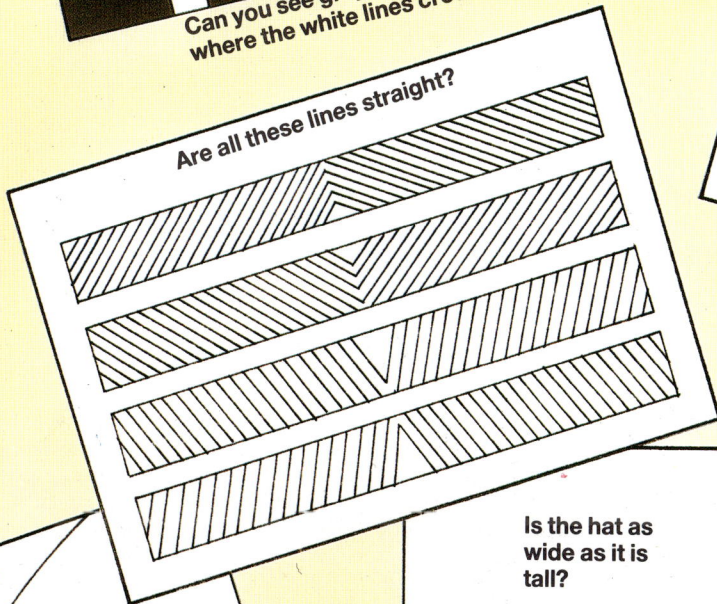

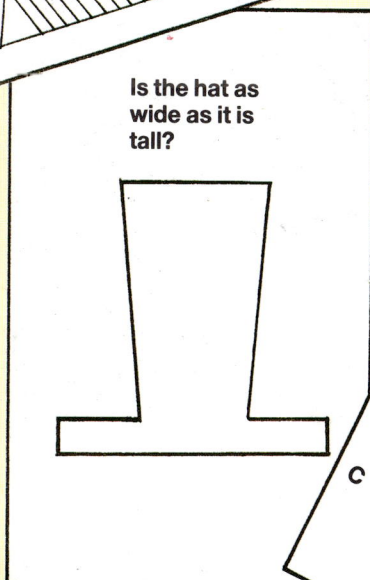

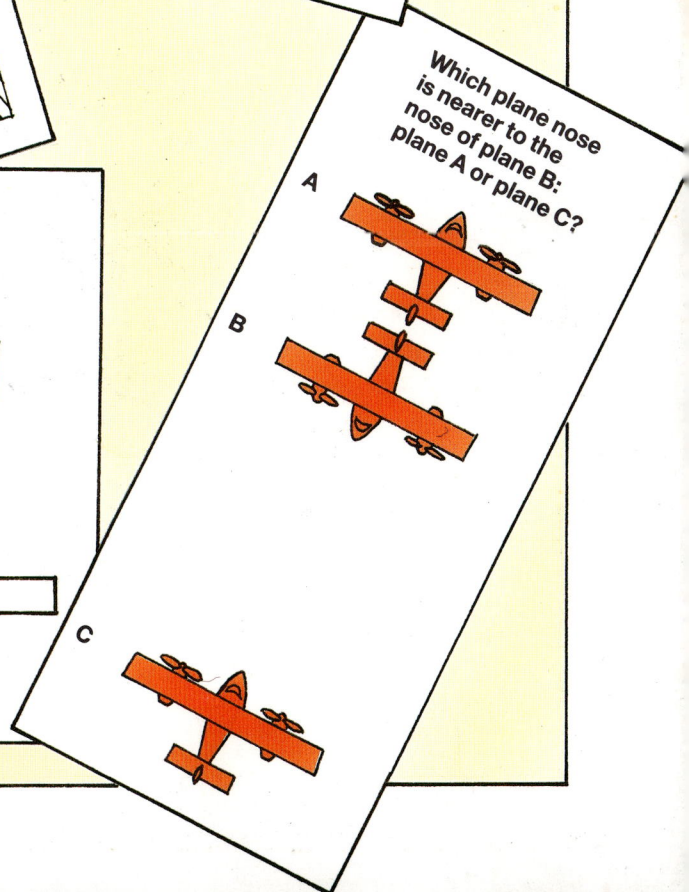

Do you think you could make this?

Can you see grey spots appearing where the white lines cross?

Which flower centre is bigger?

Are all these lines straight?

Which plane nose is nearer to the nose of plane B: plane A or plane C?

A

B

C

Is the hat as wide as it is tall?

Can you see a young lady or an old lady?

THAUMATROPES

The thaumatrope was invented in 1826 and is one of the earliest optical toys. It is a spinning disc with a picture either side.

1 Cut a disc sixty millimetres in diameter from card.

2 Punch holes near the edge of the card.

3 Thread string through the holes of the card.

4 Draw pictures on each side of the card circle. Remember to have the back picture upside down as shown.

5 Turn the strings. The two pictures will merge as you spin the disc.

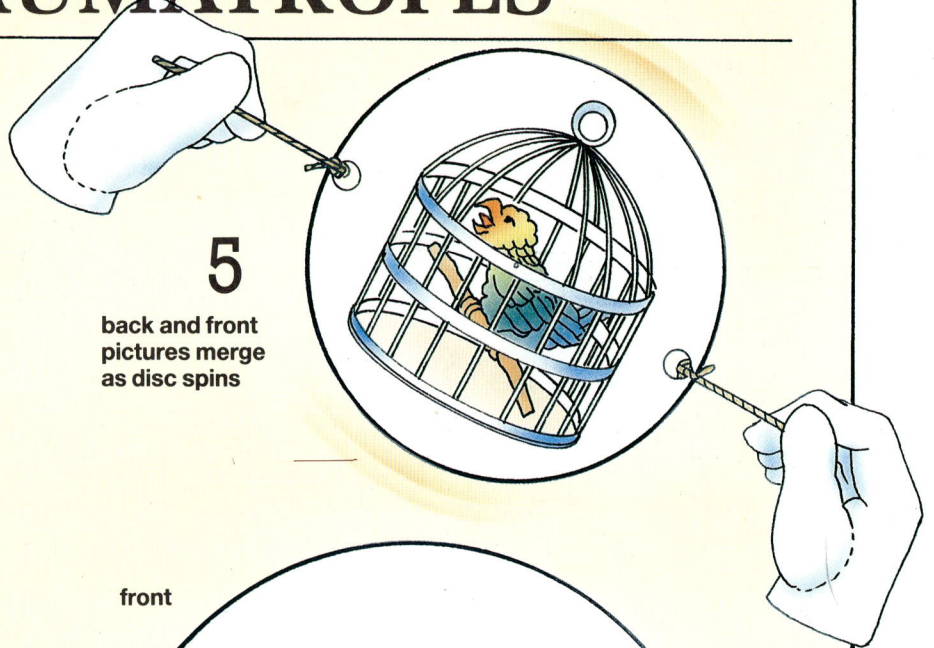

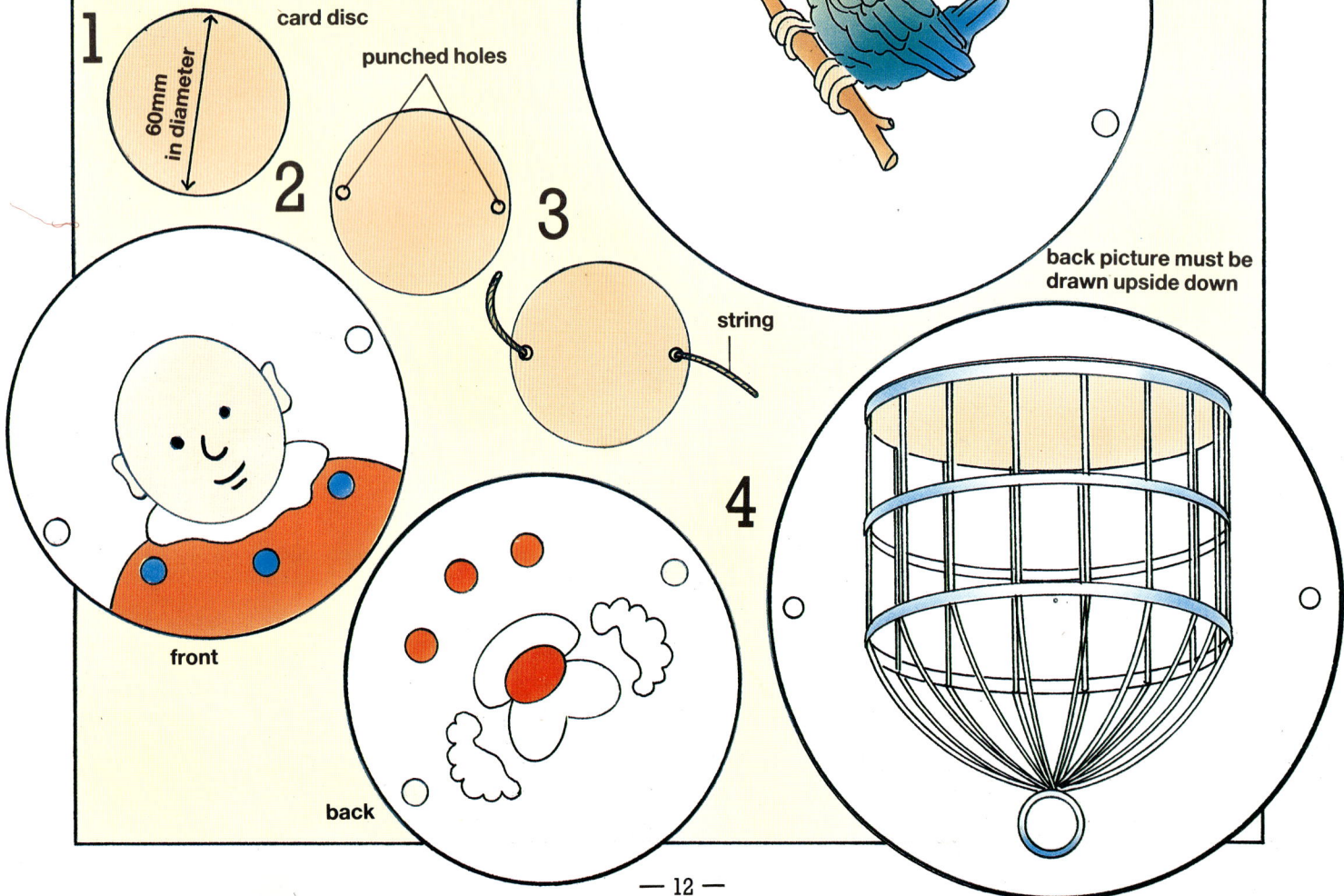

5 back and front pictures merge as disc spins

front

1 card disc

60mm in diameter

2 punched holes

3 string

back picture must be drawn upside down

front

4

back

punch holes for string

You can also use card oblongs. Here are more suggestions for designs for you to copy or trace.

card oblong

horse

and rider

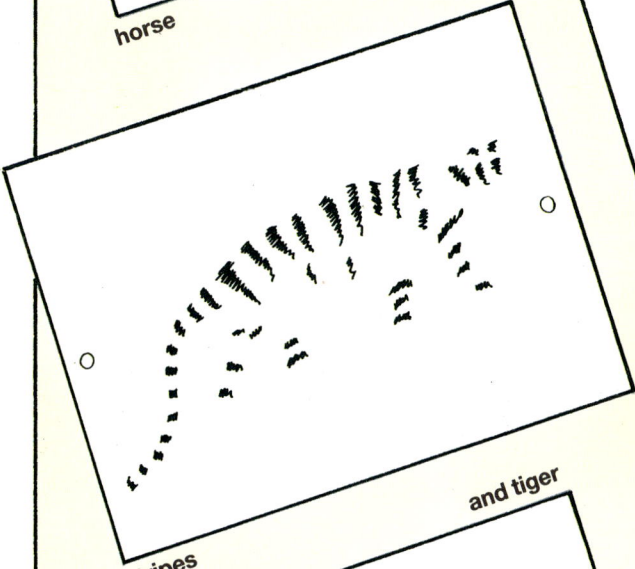

stripes

and tiger

eyes

and sunglasses

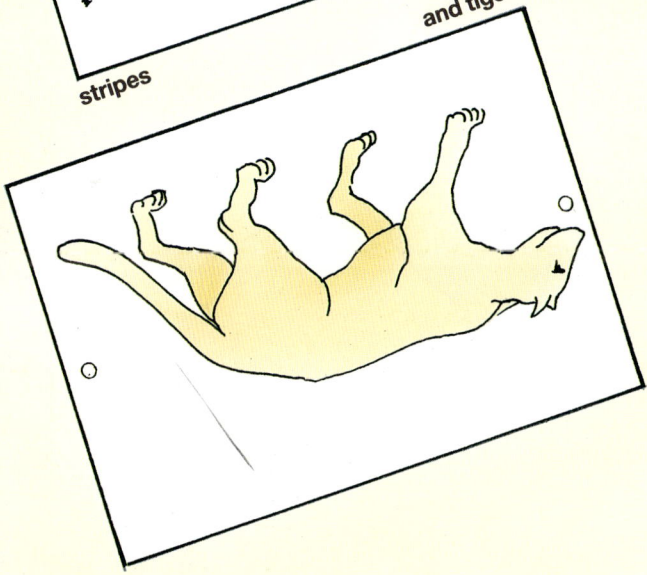

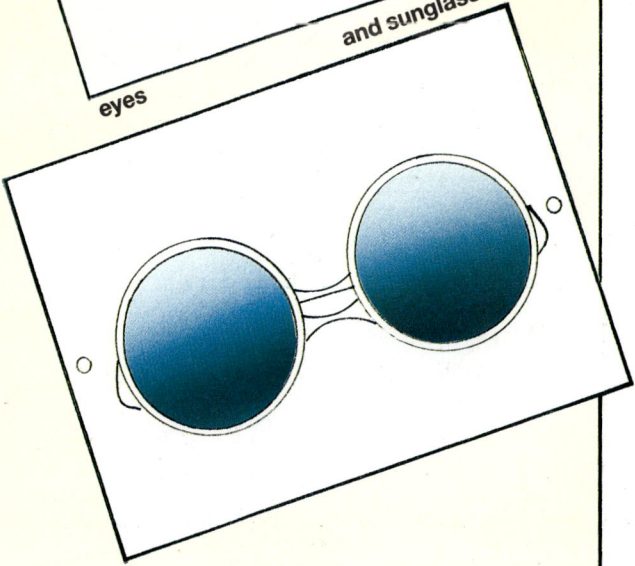

PHENAKISTOSCOPES

Joseph Antoine Plateau, a Belgian discovered an intriguing effect produced by viewing moving pictures through slits.

The device he invented was called a phenakistoscope or stroboscope. The way this works is because the brain has the ability to retain pictures for a short while. Each successive picture of the frog stays in your mind.

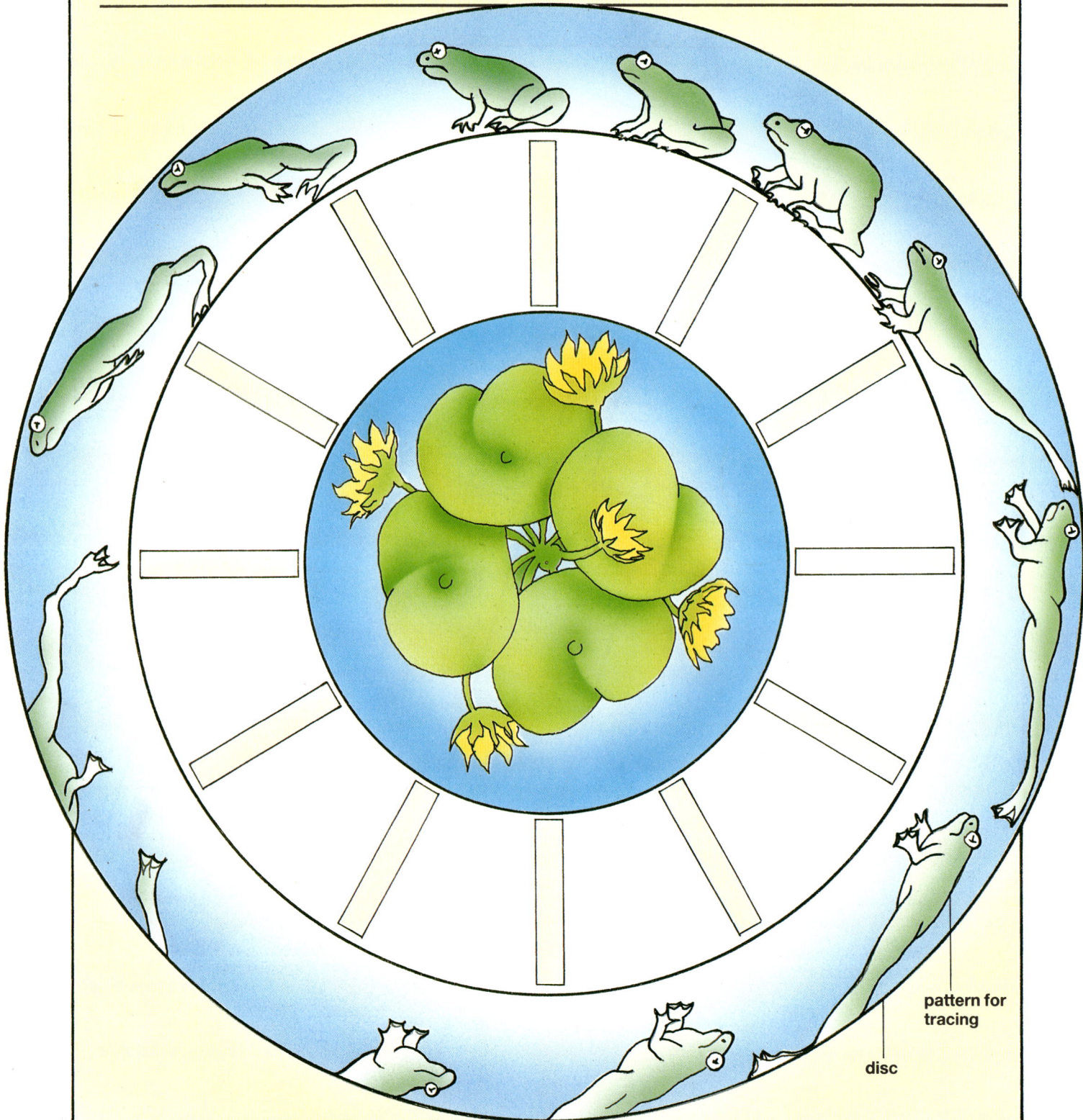

pattern for tracing

disc

1 Cut out a disc of card the same diameter as the disc on page 14.

2 Trace the pattern of leaping frogs on the opposite page. Glue it to the outer edge of your card disc. Let it dry.

3 Cut out the viewing slits with a pocket Stanley knife, as shown below.

4 Push a hat pin or nail through the disc and into a cork. Put a bead either side of the disc to make it run smoothly.

5 Hold the disc up to a mirror. Make sure there is a good light beyond you.

Twirl the disc by gently striking the edge.

Look through the slits. Watch the moving pictures in a mirror.

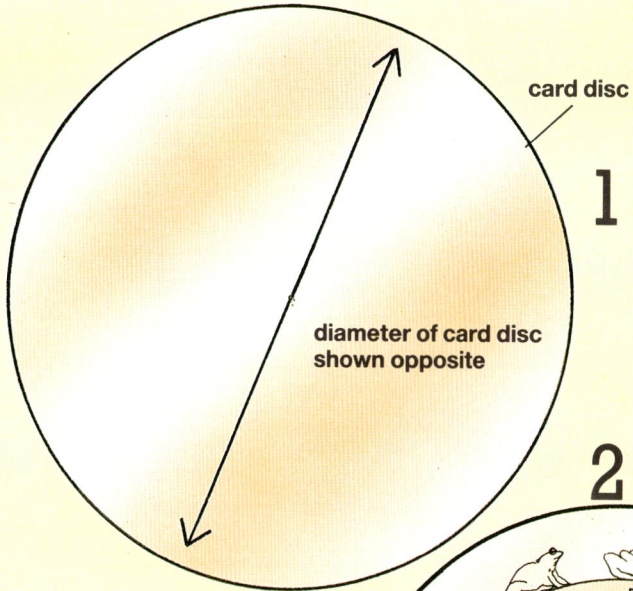

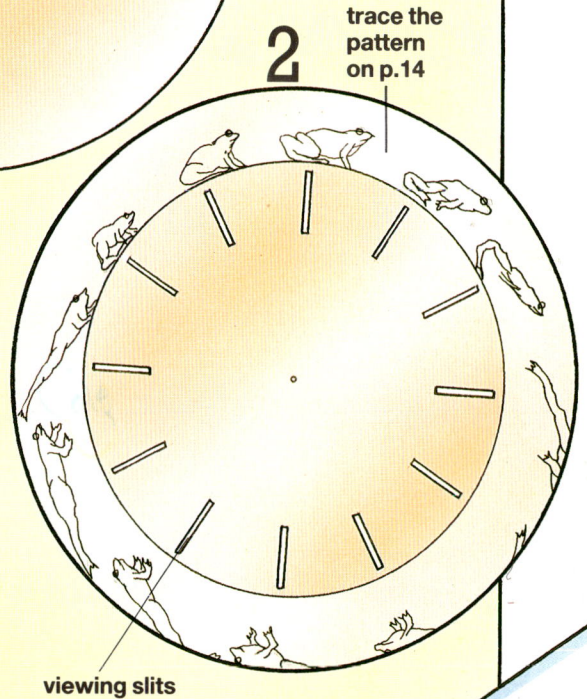

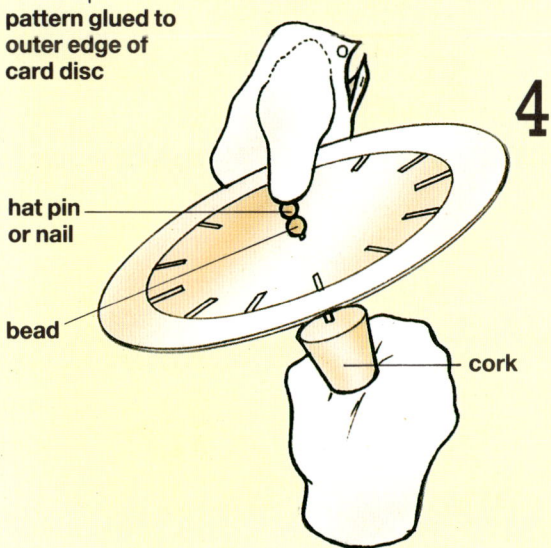

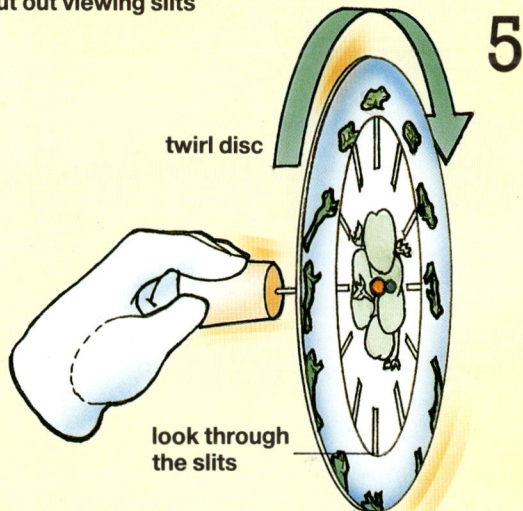

card disc

1

diameter of card disc shown opposite

2

trace the pattern on p.14

viewing slits

pocket knife

3

cut out viewing slits

pattern glued to outer edge of card disc

hat pin or nail

bead

cork

4

twirl disc

5

look through the slits

mirror

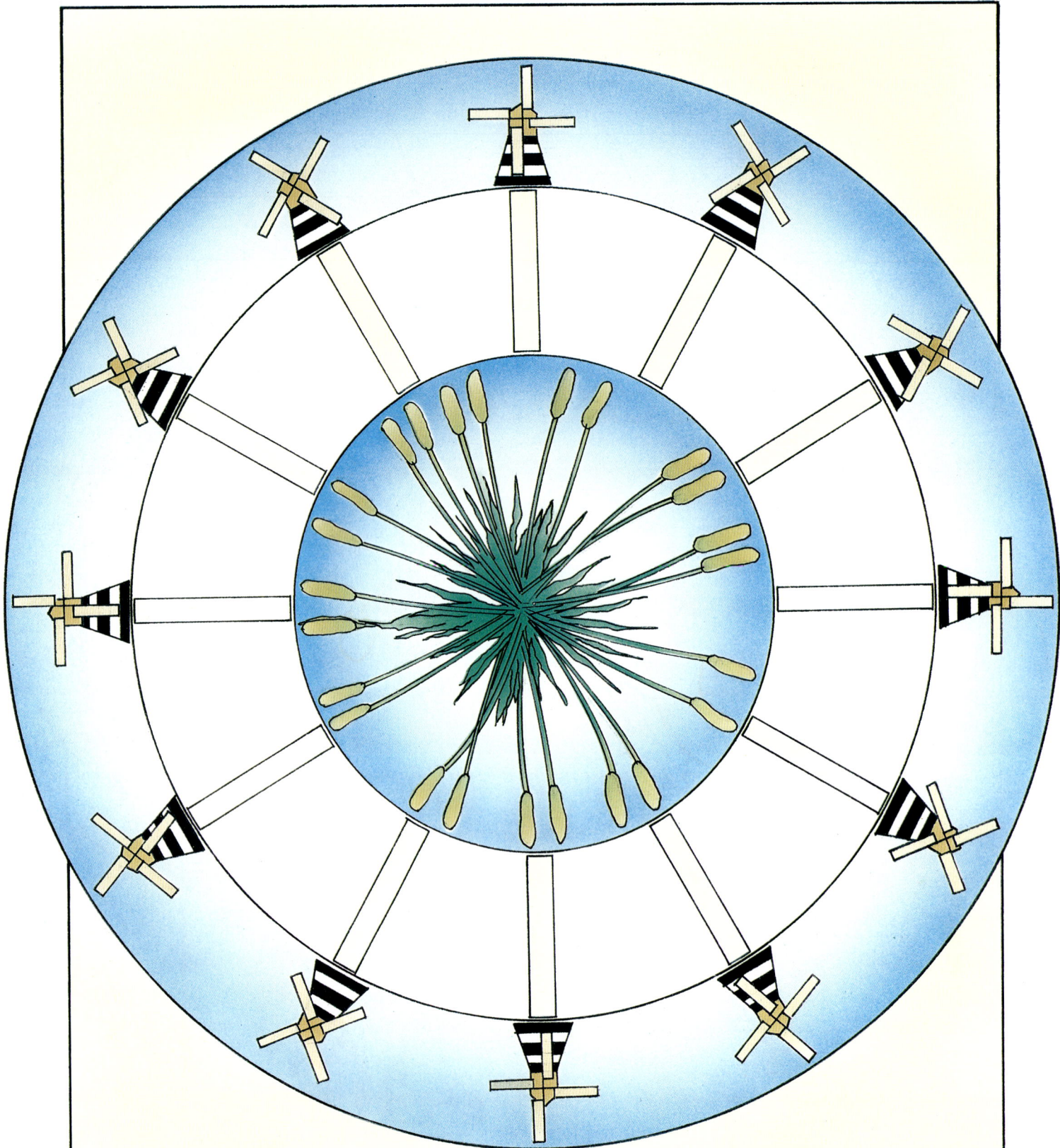

Here are two more patterns for you to trace for your phenakistoscope.

Try viewing through the slits whilst spinning the disc slowly.

Now try viewing but spin the disc quickly.

What happens?

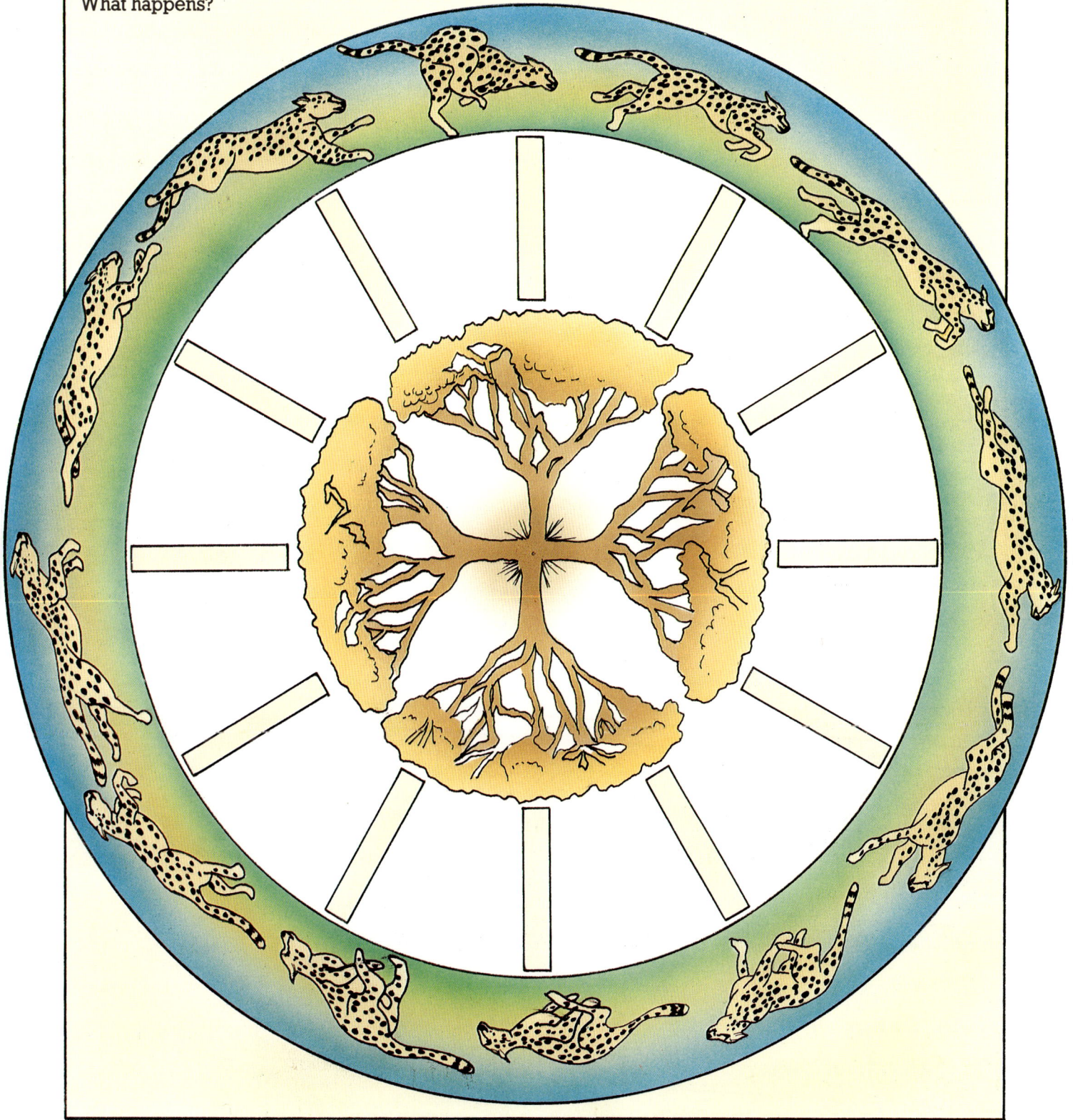

FLICK BOOKS

It is easy to make a moving action picture book. You need a story line like the one shown on the opposite page. It has 32 pictures. Copy the series of pictures shown on the opposite page onto thin card.

1 Cut out each picture. Punch two holes at the side.

2 Put them in numbered order, starting from the bottom up. Put picture number 1 on the bottom. Tie them with thin string. Bind with sticky tape.

3 Hold the book by the bound end and flick the pages from back to front with your other hand. You will see the pictures move. Make up some more books. There are some suggestions below for story lines. You make up the "in between" pictures. Keep the pictures to the right.

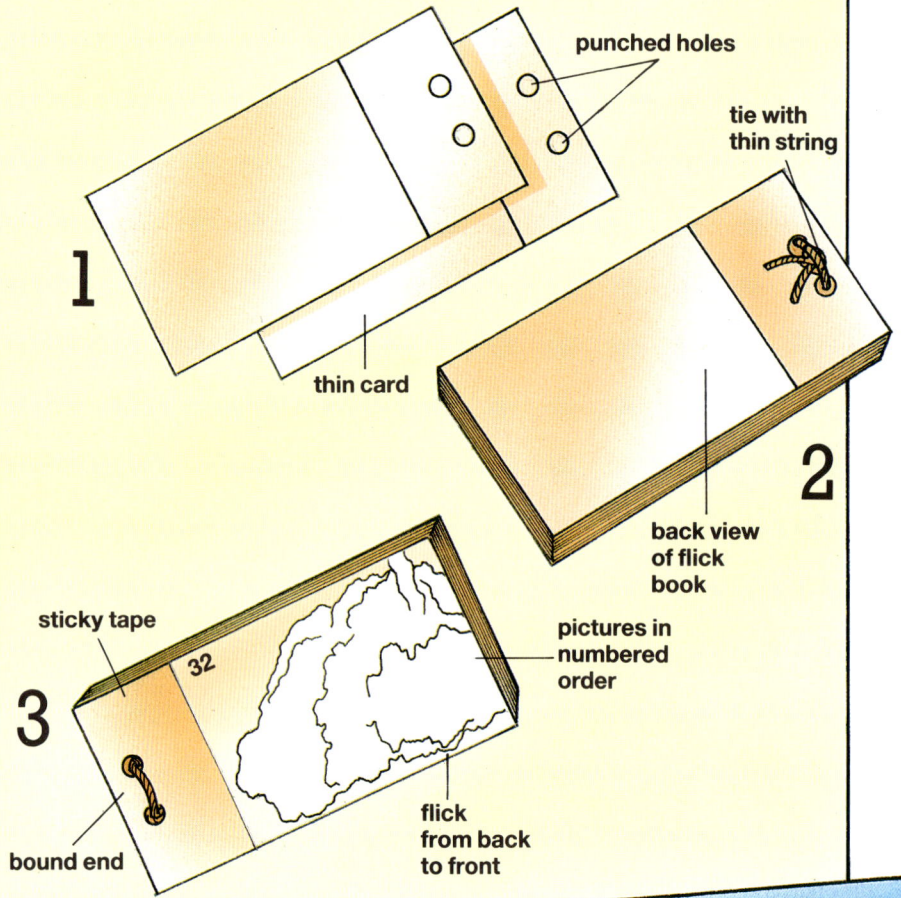

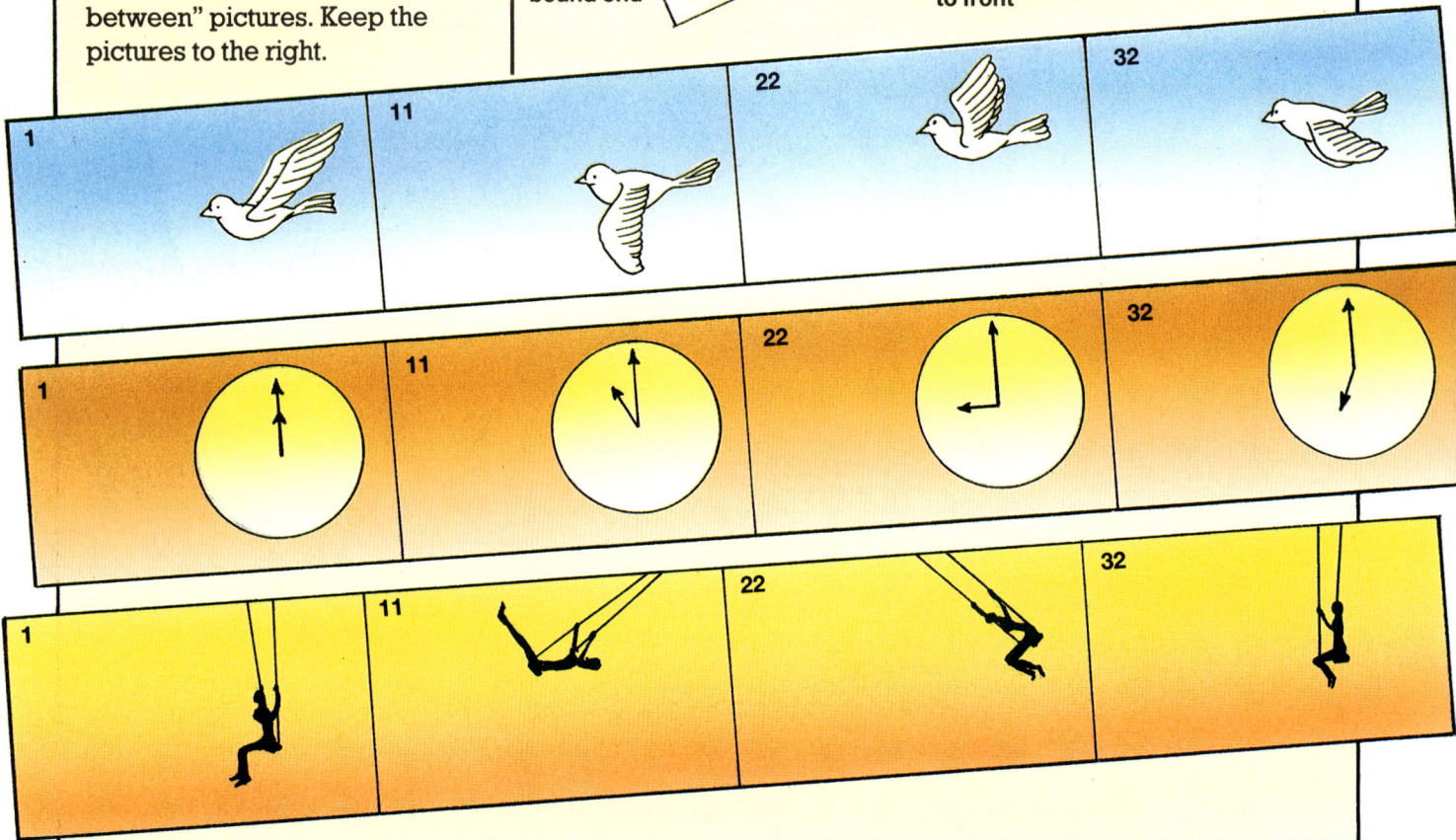

punched holes

tie with thin string

1

thin card

2

back view of flick book

pictures in numbered order

sticky tape

3

32

bound end

flick from back to front

ZOETROPES

In 1834 William George Horner, an English mathematician, invented a device that became a popular Victorian toy. It enabled the Victorians to see moving pictures. You can make a zoetrope.

1 Draw a circle of radius 87·5 millimetres (diameter 175 millimetres) on thick card. Cut out the disc.

2 Cut a thin strip of black card 560 millimetres long and 160 millimetres wide. Trace the template on the opposite page and use it to give you the spacing for the slits and tabs. The slits must be cut out with a pocket Stanley knife. You can cut the tabs with scissors.

3 Score along line AB and bend the tabs inward.

4 Glue the tabs to the card disc. Join the overlap in the card with sticky tape.

5 Fix a pin through the centre of the zoetrope (with a bead either side so that it runs smoothly) into a cork. Stand the cork in a weighted bottle full of sand or soil.

You will need a strip of figures to stick inside your zoetrope. There are strips of figures for you to trace on page 22.

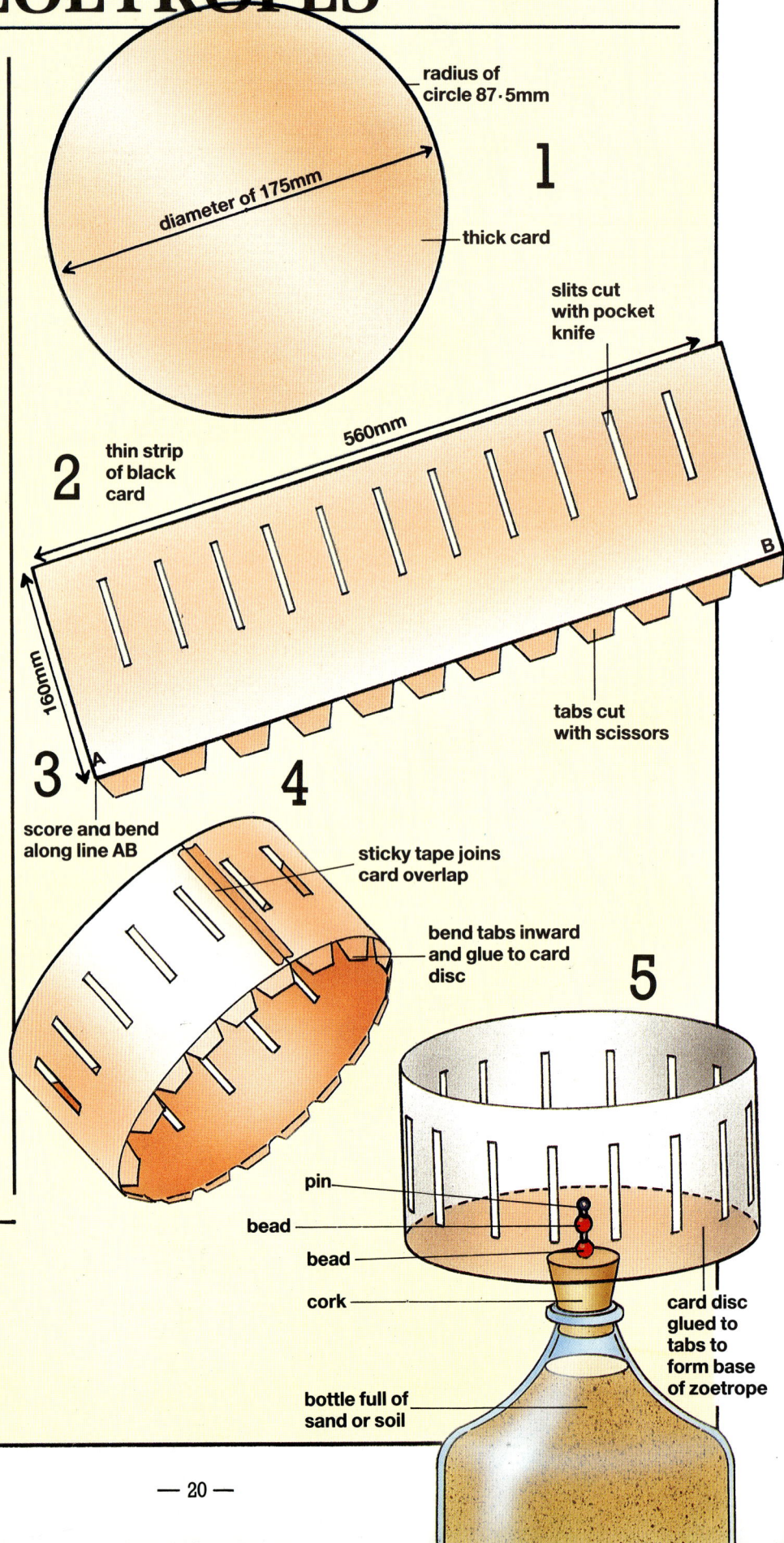

1

radius of circle 87·5mm

diameter of 175mm

thick card

2 thin strip of black card

560mm

160mm

slits cut with pocket knife

tabs cut with scissors

B

3 score and bend along line AB

A

4

sticky tape joins card overlap

bend tabs inward and glue to card disc

5

pin

bead

bead

cork

card disc glued to tabs to form base of zoetrope

bottle full of sand or soil

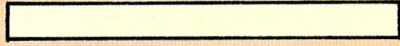

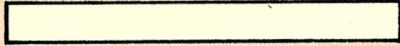

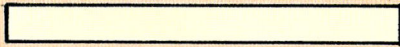

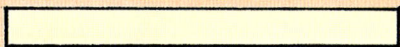

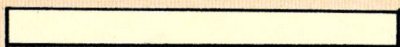

**template for
tracing**

1 Trace these figures below. Join AA to BB, CC to DD to make a continuous strip. Notice the movement is from right to left. Stick the strip in your zoetrope so that it runs round the edge of the drum just beneath the slits.

2 Spin the zoetrope. Peep through the slits. Can you see the figures moving? If you sit back from the zoetrope you will get a better picture.

3 There are two more strips for tracing opposite.

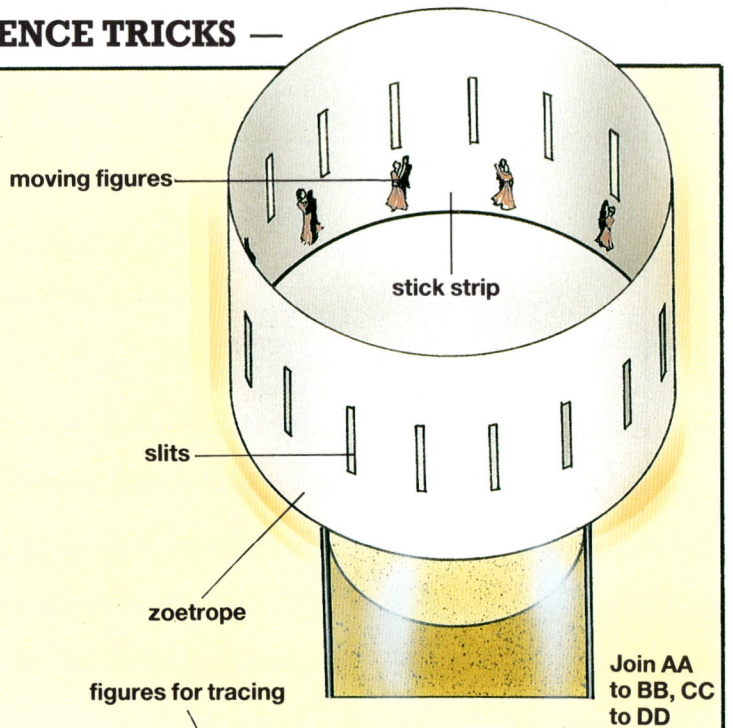

moving figures

stick strip

slits

zoetrope

figures for tracing

Join AA to BB, CC to DD

A

A

B

C

B

C

D

D

CURVES FROM CIRCLES

1 Take a pair of compasses and mark two points A and B, 100 millimetres apart.

2 Draw circles from each point. Increase the radius of each circle by 10 millimetres at a time.

3 Draw in ellipses as shown. Can you construct more?

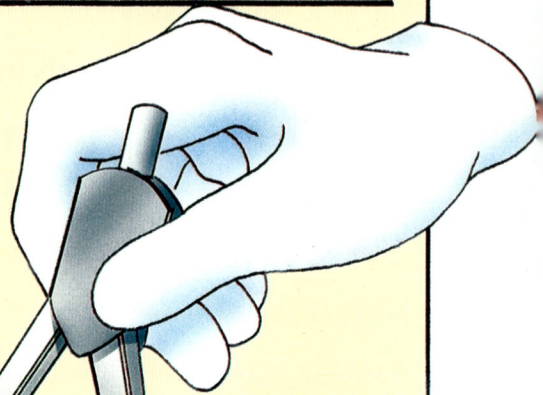

circle radius to increase by 10mm at a time

pair of compasses

ellipses

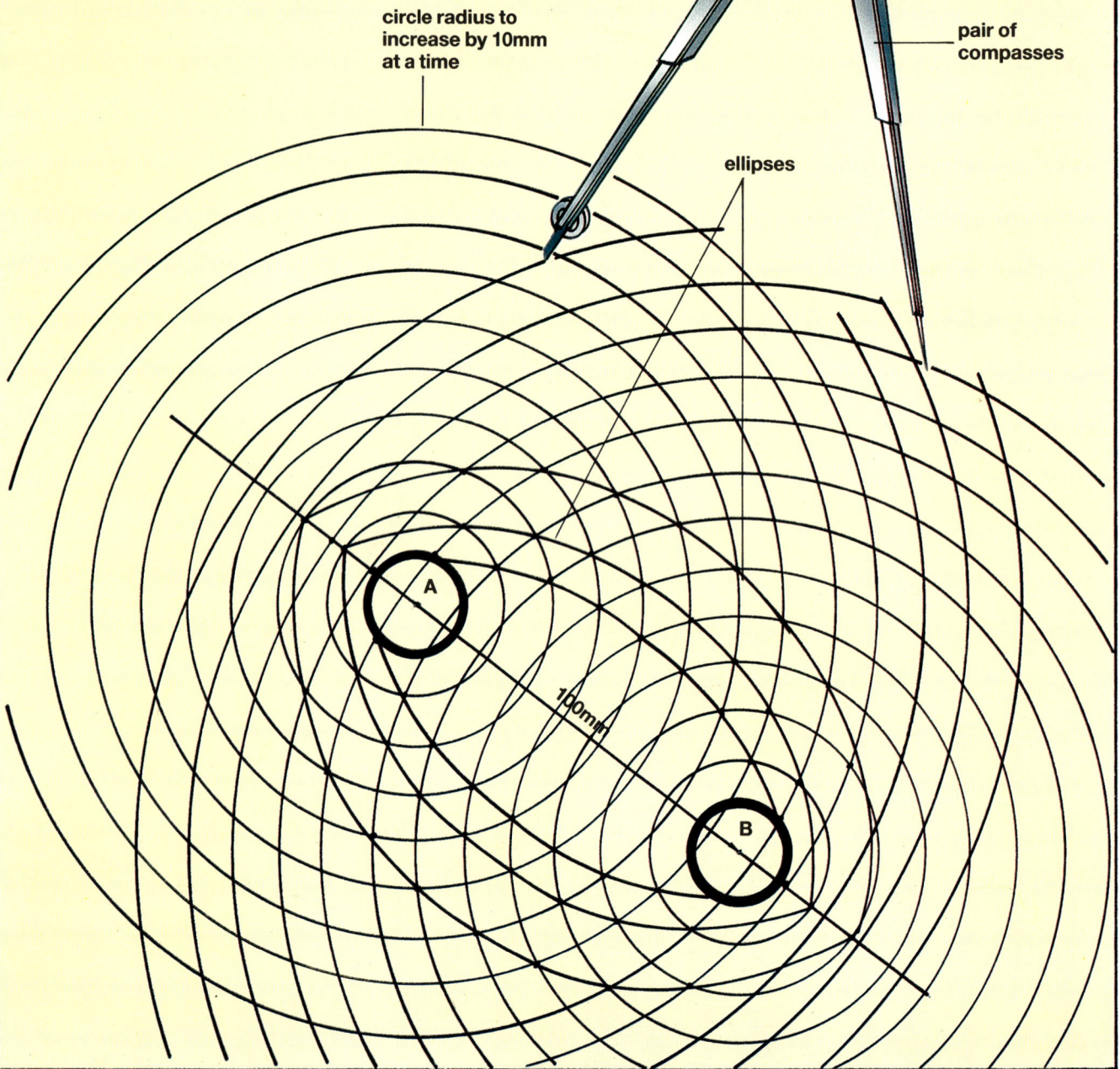

A

B

100mm

You can make all sorts of patterns. Here are two examples. The patterning shows the ellipses.

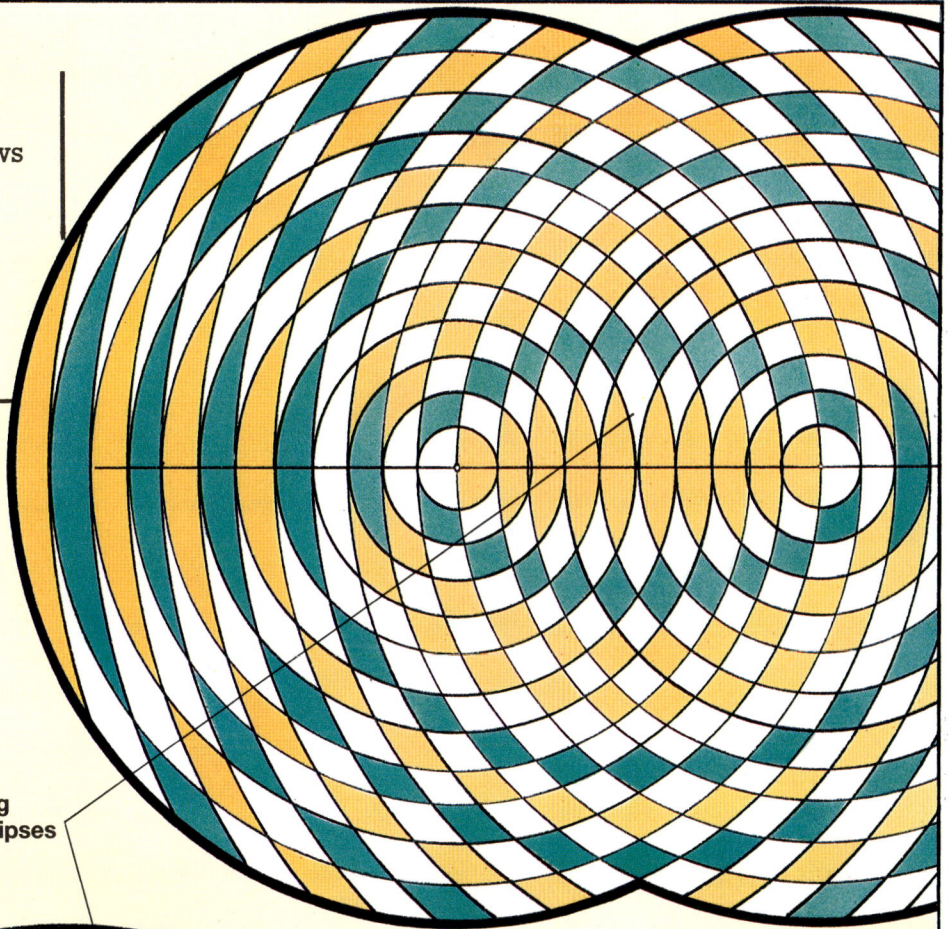

Try making other patterns by using different colours and choosing other parts of the design to colour in.

patterning
shows ellipses

CIRCLES FROM LINES

1 Take a pair of compasses again and draw a circle. Mark every 10 degrees around the circle using a protractor. You will end up with 36 marks.

2 Draw a line across the circle connecting two marks, A B. Take the next set of marks, C, D and connect them. Notice C is below A and D is above B. Repeat the pattern all round the circle.

You will find that you make a new circle at the centre using your straight lines.

3 Draw a new line closer to the centre E F. Draw the next line G H, again with G below E and H above F. Continue as before.

You will now make a new circle at the centre.

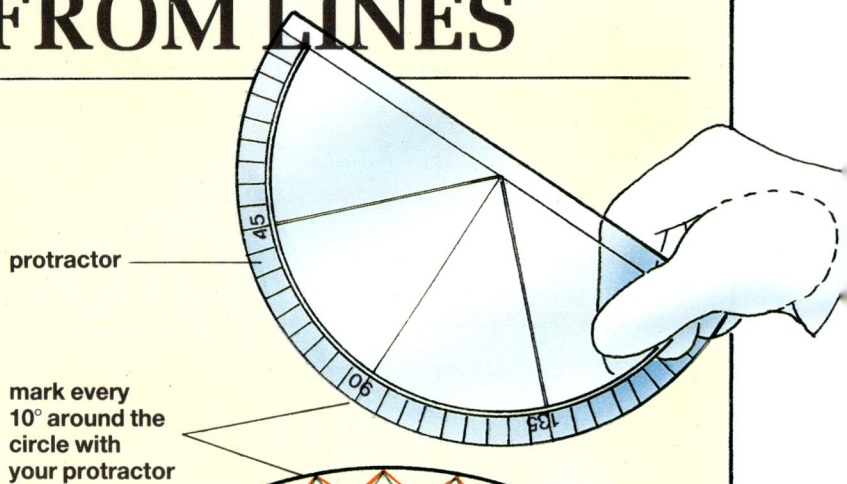

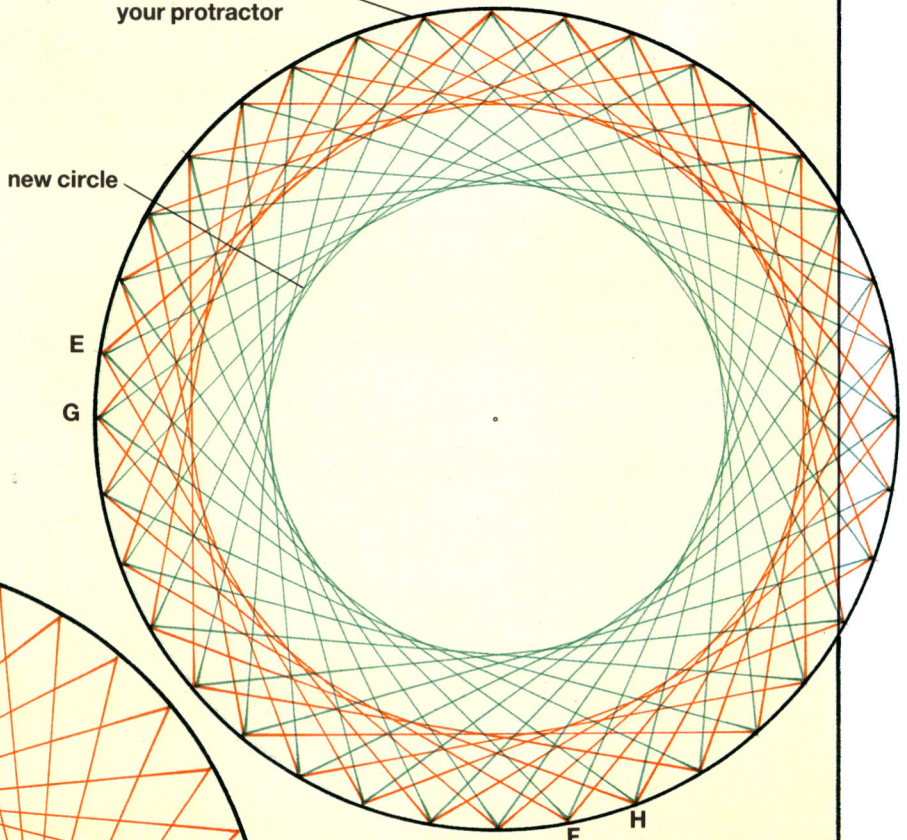

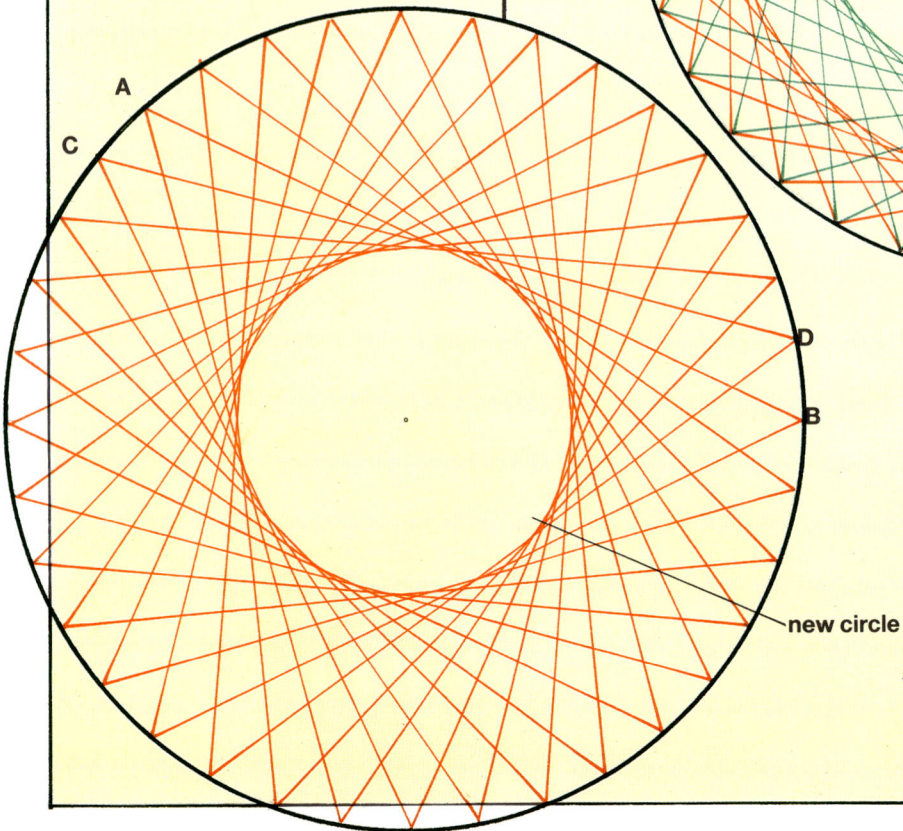

protractor

mark every 10° around the circle with your protractor

new circle

E
G

F H

A
C

D
B

new circle

4 Draw a circle. Mark every 15 degrees around the circle using a protractor. You will end up with 24 marks. From every mark around the circle draw straight lines to every other mark. You will make the pattern below. It contains lots of new circles made from straight lines.

mark every 15°
around the circle
with your protractor

from every mark
draw straight
lines to every
other mark

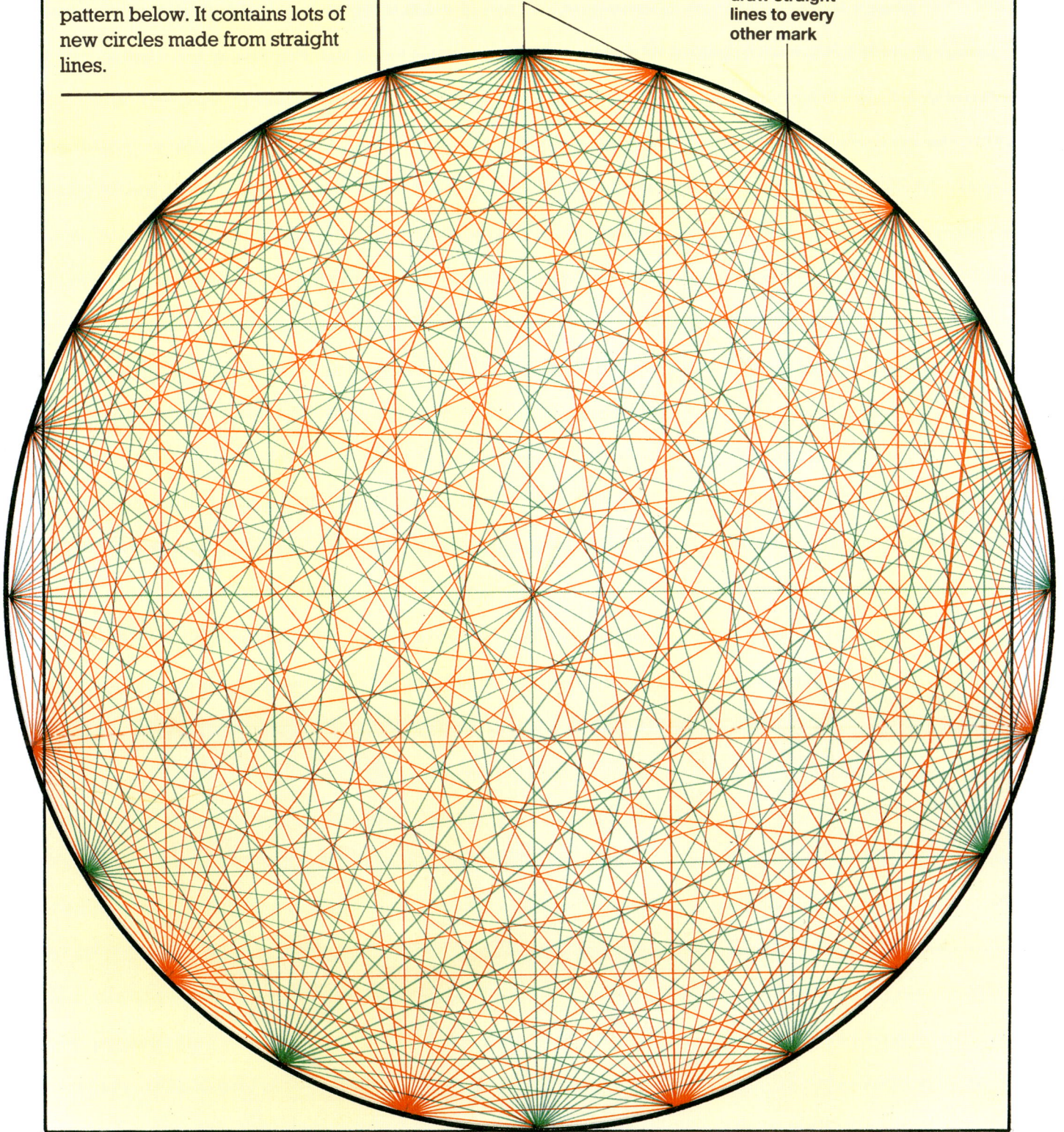

MORE CURVES

A SINGLE CURVE

1 Draw an angle ABC. Mark off 5 millimetre sections on each line.

2 Draw lines DH, EI, FJ, GK and so on. You will find that you make a curve.

Try longer lines. Try changing the size of the angle.

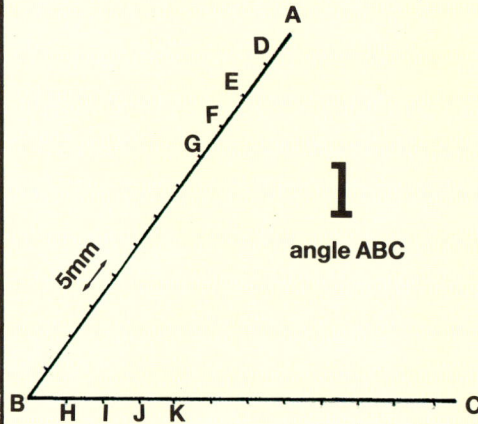

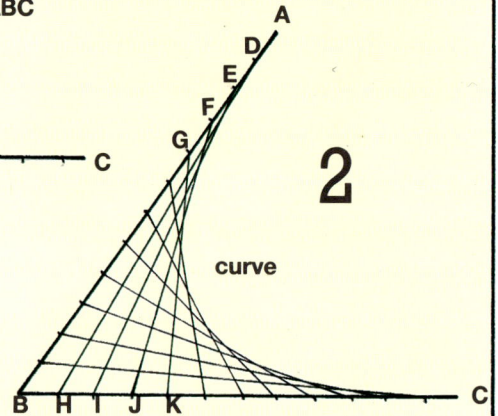

A DOUBLE CURVE

Draw a circle. Use a protractor to mark every 5 degrees. You should have 72 marks. Draw lines AB, BD, CF, DH, EJ, and so on. Each line drawn is one mark beyond the previous starting mark and two marks on from the previous ending mark.

The result is a double curve.

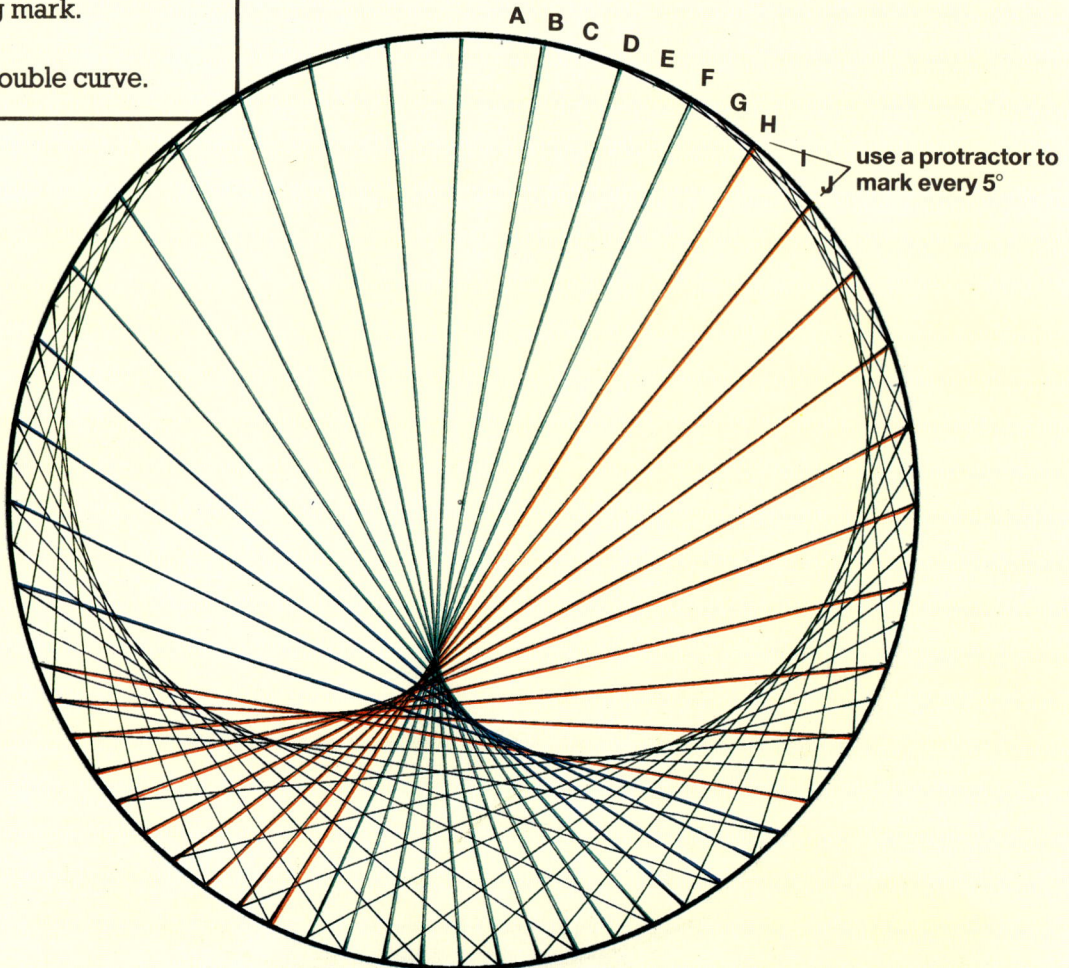

1 angle ABC

5mm

2 curve

use a protractor to mark every 5°

double curve

A NUMBER OF CURVES

Use a protractor to draw five angles of 72 degrees around the circle centre at A.

Mark off 5 millimetre sections on each line. Draw lines between the marks as for the single curve on the previous page.

protractor

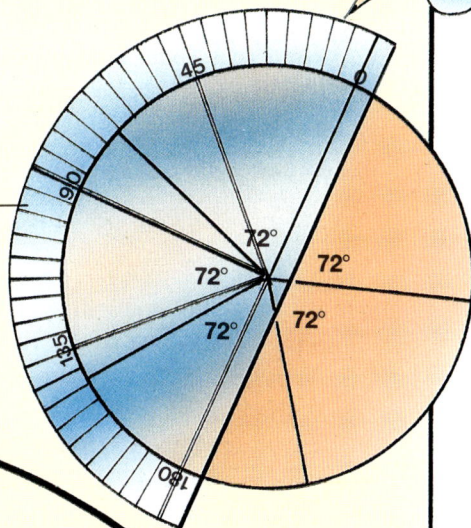

curves

CURVE STITCHING

Using a needle or pins and darning wool many of the curved patterns that you have been drawing can be picked out on card to make a picture. Lightly draw your pattern first. Then make it using coloured wool.

Draw a square on card with 160 millimetre sides. Mark every 10 millimetres around the square. Connect these marks to make a single curve at each corner as described on the previous page.

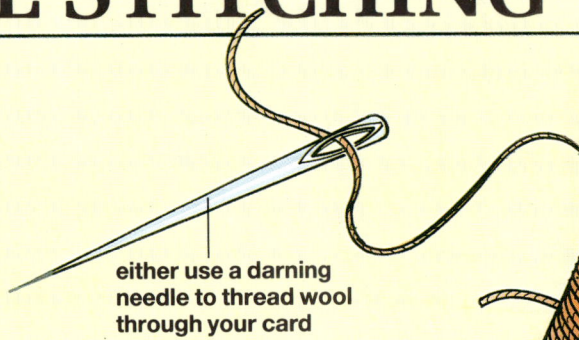

either use a darning needle to thread wool through your card

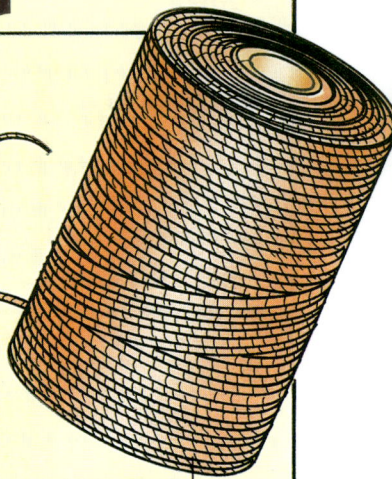

overlay pattern on card with coloured wool

bobbin of coloured wool

or use pins round card edge to hold wool

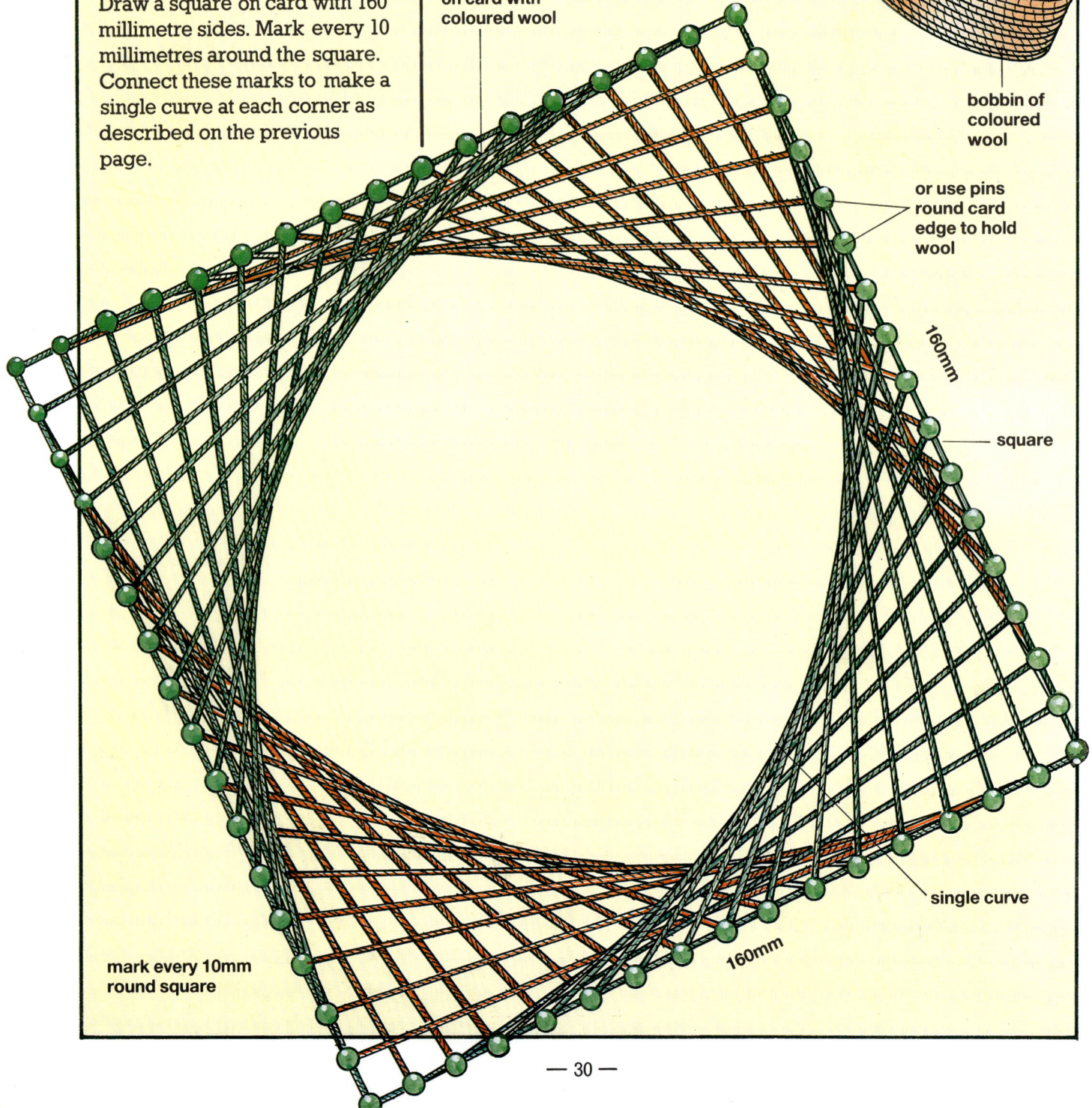

160mm

square

single curve

160mm

mark every 10mm round square

SPIRAL

Trace the spiral below onto card. Mark the 25 points. Join each point to the 24 others.

The pattern you get is the nautilus shell found in tropical waters. Look around for other spiral patterns. Garden snails, pine cones and spiral staircases are more examples.

Again, you could overlay the pattern with wool as shown in the picture on the right.

pattern of
nautilus shell

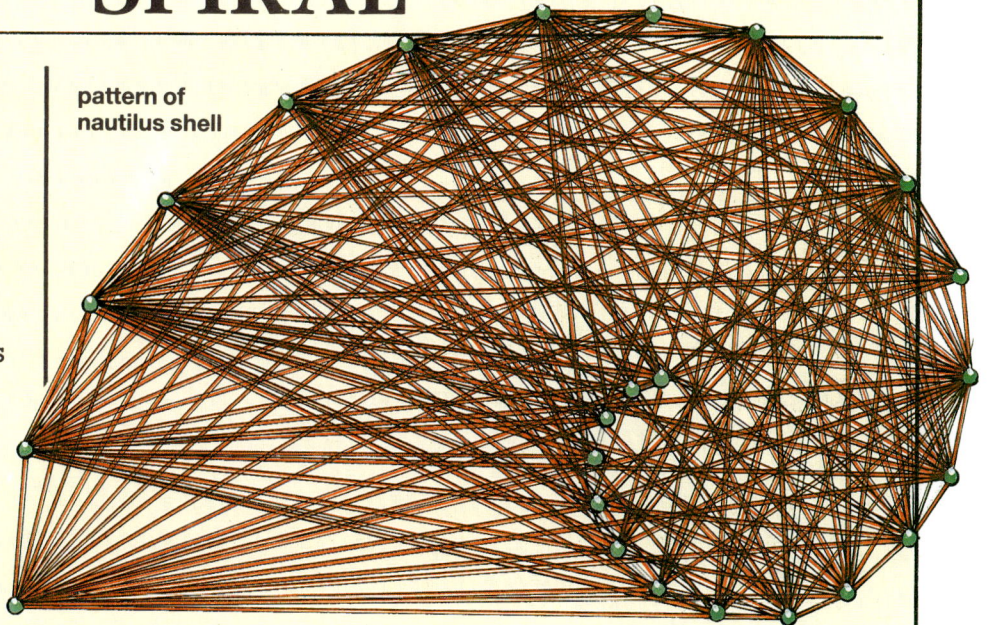

spiral for
tracing

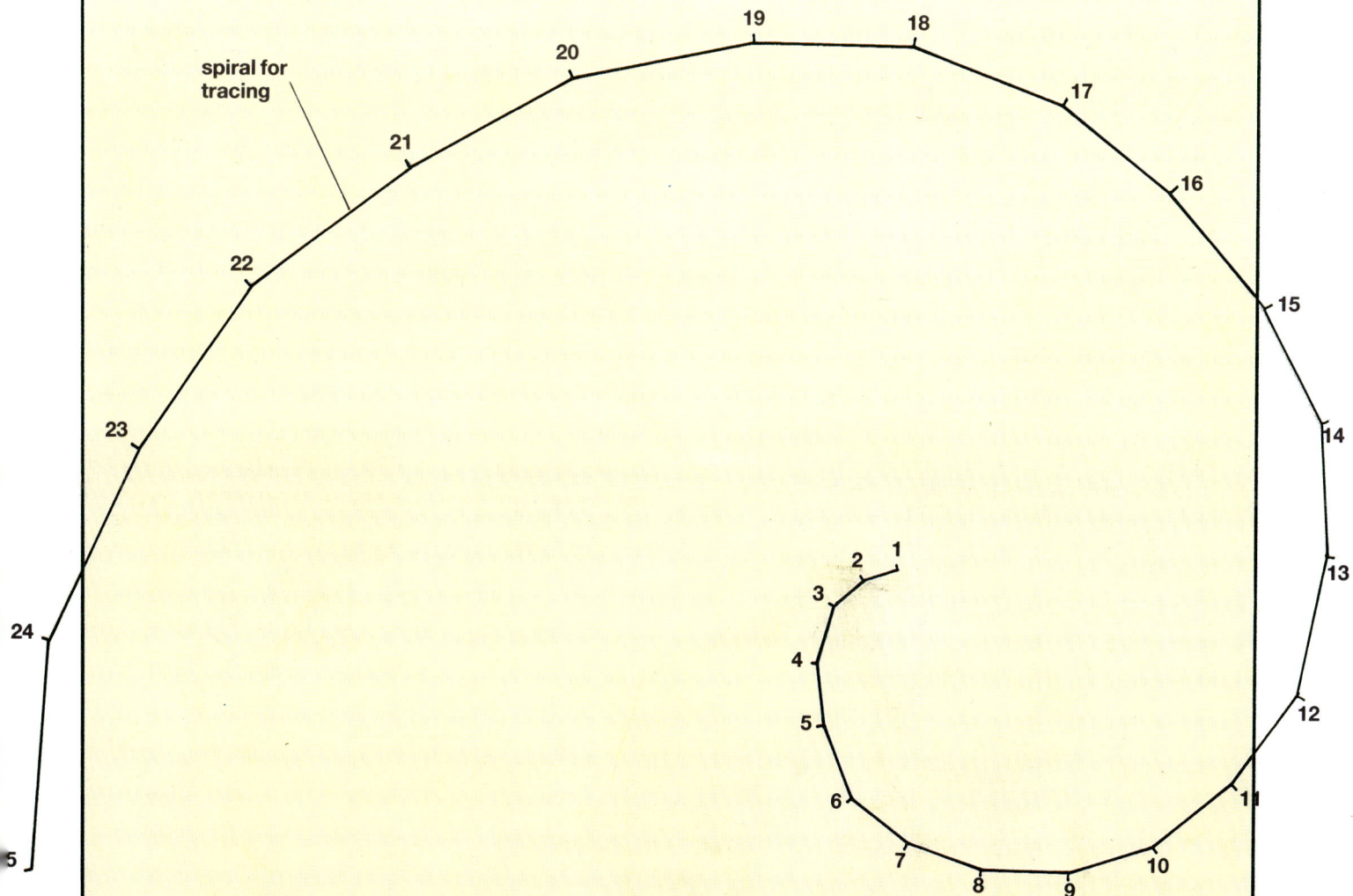

NOTES FOR PARENTS AND TEACHERS

The activities described in this book vary in the degree of skill required by children but all the activities are relatively easy to do, and should be well within the capabilities of children in the 7–13 age range. There is a strong scientific or mathematical basis to each of the activities. For children the fun of making and doing is all. For parents and teachers the following notes may be of interest in making the most of what lies beyond all these things to do.

Pages 3 – 23 These pages are concerned in some way or other with light and with the way we perceive things.

Children are learning that:
- light travels in straight lines
- light can be made to change direction
- shiny surfaces form images
- light can be reflected
- the brain can retain images to create an impression of movement.

All of these concepts are developed by carrying out the simple activities suggested. There is much that children can learn from investigations with mirrors.

Pages 3, 4 and 5 These are concerned with the way shiny mirror surfaces reflect well, and with reflective symmetry. They show how mirror images can be completed in both a horizontal and a vertical plane.

Pages 6 and 7 These show how putting two or more mirrors together can multiply the reflections and create a 'kaleidoscopic' effect.

Pages 8 and 9 These show how light can be bent through an angle of 90 degrees using a mirror and how this effect is put into use to produce a periscope.

Pages 10 and 11 Carrying out the activities on Page 10 results in each eye receiving a separate image. The brain merges these together so that we see one composite picture. Page 11 illustrates how visual images can deceive.

Pages 12 and 13 The brain can retain images for a short while. This ability is made use of in the spinning picture toy called the thaumatrope.

Pages 14 – 17 Again the ability of the brain to retain images for a short while is made use of in the phenakistoscope to give an impression of continuous movement.

Pages 18 – 19 The flick book reinforces the way we retain images, as we see a rapidly moving succession of pictures. This creates the illusion of movement.

Pages 20 – 23 This section completes the work on light and optical toys by showing how to make a zoetrope. The retention of images by the brain is made use of in a toy which was a precursor of modern cinema.

Pages 24 – 31 Here seeing is believing. We can use straight lines and circles to produce curves. This section is concerned with mathematical exploration. Children are learning that mathematics has pattern which is probably one of the most important things about mathematics.

They are learning that:
- straight lines can be used to produce circles
- chords drawn to a circle produce an inner circle called an envelope
- there are ellipses
- there is pattern in mathematics.

Pages 24 and 25 Introduce children to ellipses and pattern making.

Pages 26 and 27 Show how drawing chords to a circle produces an inner circle which mathematicians call an envelope.

Pages 28 and 29 Develop the idea of getting curves from straight lines.

Pages 30 and 31 Show how wool can be used to make a picture commonly known as curved stitching. On Page 31 children can find out how straight lines can be used to develop the idea of making a spiral.

PRINTED IN BELGIUM BY
proost
INTERNATIONAL BOOK PRODUCTION